The Shepherd's Daughter

An In-Depth Study of the Twenty-third Psalm

DEBBIE DUPUY

Publishing Designs, Inc.

Huntsville, Alabama

Publishing Designs, Inc.
P.O. Box 3241
Huntsville, Alabama 35810

Editors: Peggy Coulter, Debra Wright
Cover and page design: CrosslinCreative.net
Cover image: GoodSalt.com
Interior images: iStock, Creative Market

Printed in the United States of America

Publisher's Cataloging in Publication Data

Dupuy, Debbie, 1961—

The Shepherd's Daughter

196 pp.

Preliminary study, 14 chapters, and study questions

ISBN 978-1-945127-17-5

1. Psalm 23—Application. 2. Jesus, the Good Shepherd. 3. Sheep parallels—Christian women.

Title

248.8

Contents

SECTION 1

Counting Your Sheep
The Countdown: Before You Begin

SECTION 2

Sheep to Sheep
What David Says as a Sheep

—— **SECTION 3** ——
Sheep to Shepherd
Sheep Trials and Shepherd Provisions

To the Shepherd of my heart,
Who in a late-night discovery,
assured me that I am not alone.

To Destini and Mila, my beautiful granddaughters—
may you grow up knowing
there is no greater reward
and no deeper satisfaction
than being the Shepherd's daughters.

To my family and friends—I love you.
And especially Daddy,
whose dark, cloudy days, taught me who I am.

Introduction

Dear reader, there is a difference in knowing the Twenty-third Psalm and knowing the Shepherd of the Twenty-third Psalm. I learned this truth during my dad's long illness—a season of my life in which each day brought new challenges. I could quote the Twenty-third Psalm, but I never really knew what it meant until I began to study.

Knowing the Shepherd is comforting when you understand what He does for His sheep. Being close to the Shepherd will uphold you through the harrowing events of life. And being led by the Shepherd will make all the difference when you face difficulties and need His assurance.

Reciting and Committing the Twenty-third Psalm to Memory

Learn to recite the Twenty-third Psalm from memory, and repeat the palm before each chapter. The more familiar you are with the psalm, the closer you will be to the Shepherd. I cannot recite one verse without thinking about what it means to me as the Shepherd's daughter.

I'm so excited for you because I believe that is how you will feel when you finish the study!

The Lord, the Shepherd of His People
A Psalm of David

The Lord is my shepherd; I shall not want.
He makes me to lie down in green pastures;
He leads me beside the still waters. He restores my soul;
He leads me in the paths of righteousness for His name's sake.
Yea, though I walk through the valley of the shadow of death,
I will fear no evil; for You are with me;
Your rod and Your staff, they comfort me.

You prepare a table before me in the presence of my enemies;
You anoint my head with oil; my cup runs over.
Surely goodness and mercy shall follow me all the days of my life;
And I will dwell in the house of the Lord forever.

—Psalm 23

What to Expect

As you read these pages, you will discover the benefits of being the Shepherd's daughter. Here is an illustration of what you will learn:

An old preacher was at a benefit dinner. Also in attendance was a renowned actor who was always asked to grace the gathering with his eloquent words before the meal was consumed. He chose to quote the Twenty-third Psalm.

He stood with an arrogant demeanor and began to quote the ever-popular psalm. When he finished the crowd applauded, and he sat down with a pride-filled disposition.

Then, in the corner of the room, an old gray-haired stately figure rose to his feet as the people hushed the gala. He blared, "My name is preacher Tom Rawlins, and I am a hundred years old today. I would also like to say something if I may." Obviously respecting the age of this humble man, the people obliged.

Preacher Rawlins gathered his senses for a moment, took a deep breath of air into his lungs and began: "The Lord is my shepherd, I shall not want . . ."

As he ended the last verse, tears streaking his wrinkled face, he sat down. One could have heard a feather hit the floor. The only sounds heard were those of three hundred people quietly weeping to themselves.

The actor was embarrassed and appalled because he did not get such a response. He foolishly rushed over to the old preacher's table and quickly attacked, "I've been acting and giving speeches for over thirty years, and I have never had a response like the one I saw here today. I quoted the Twenty-third Psalm just as you did. What makes you so different from me?"

The stately old preacher raised his eyes to the vibrant actor in reply, "Son, you quoted the Twenty-third Psalm, and you know the psalm well. But son, I know the Shepherd of the Twenty-third Psalm."

Psalm 23 reminds us of the wonderful provision, protection, and preservation the Shepherd supplies for His children. It also foreshadows the blessings provided by our Good Shepherd Himself, Jesus Christ.

As we begin our study, here are some points to consider:

- We will explore the habits of sheep.

- We will examine closely what a good shepherd provides for his sheep and how he cares for them.

- We will consider the meaning of each verse as it relates to the relationship the shepherd has with his sheep.

- We will apply spiritual truths for our lives as we consider the meaning of each verse.

- We will pause and think about the material presented and move past knowing scripture to applying scripture. We will take time to answer the questions and read the applications. Those applications will help to give us strength for this journey called life.

- We will complete the homework to help us deepen our relationship with the Good Shepherd. The homework encourages meditation and helps us ponder and internalize certain applications from each chapter.

This study should become so special that you will think of your Shepherd as a trusted friend who knows you. You will spend time with Him and listen as He speaks to you from His word. I want you to experience the familiarity of knowing your Shepherd is near because you listen to His voice.

The sheep hear his voice; and he calls his own sheep by name and leads them out. And when he brings out his own sheep, he goes before them; and the sheep follow him, for they know his voice.

—John 10:3–4

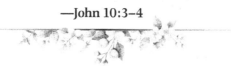

Isn't this how the writer describes our Shepherd for us in Psalm 23—with startling familiarity. He is secure in knowing the love and care of His Shepherd.

As we study this amazing passage, my prayer is that you too will come to think of yourself as the Shepherd's daughter, because in that role you will understand how much the Good Shepherd loves and cares for you. My prayer is that you will come to say: *The Lord is my Shepherd and that's all I will ever want.*

—Debbie, the Shepherd's daughter

Counting Your Sheep

The Countdown:
Before You Begin

THE COUNTDOWN:
Before You Begin

The Countdown

1 Late-Night Discoveries

Recite the Twenty-third Psalm.
At the end, add, "Oh, the benefits of being the Shepherd's daughter."

As I sat in a dark hospital room while my dad was sleeping, I remember feeling hopeless. The tightness in my chest made it hard to breathe. I was overwhelmed because of all the uncertainty swirling around in my head. I remember thinking, what is going to happen? How is this going to work out? What are my sister and I going to do? This is when I experienced a "late-night discovery."

It started in early spring. My girls were performing in a school play. One was a cow and the other was Cinderella. I, of course, was in the audience, enjoying every minute of it. My phone rang, and I stepped outside to answer it. That call stopped everything! My sister had found Dad lying on the floor. "We have called an ambulance," she said, "and we are headed to the hospital in Birmingham. Please hurry!"

The medical staff in the emergency room quickly diagnosed the problem—a stroke. That first trip to the hospital was only the beginning. After his stroke, he went to rehab—twice. But then came all the complications: pneumonia, heart failure, kidney failure, and depression. It was a constant battle between his frail body and his will.

At one point during his illness, Dad told me that he felt thirty years old in his mind, but his body told him otherwise. I can only imagine how difficult it must have been for him. He had always been active, but now his tiny body stooped in a wheelchair. His left side was paralyzed.

It was in that hospital room, after several hospital stays, that a feeling of defeat came crashing down on me because there were so many decisions to make and so many thoughts were racing in my mind. I felt overwhelmed.

Have you ever felt overwhelmed by a season of unforeseen circumstances? Explain how it made you feel.

Supplies for the Needy

I always brought a notebook, pen, small flashlight, and my Bible to the hospital to use while Dad slept. I also took a little book by Philip Keller, *A Shepherd Looks at Psalm 23*.

I had decided to read the book, take notes, and perhaps write some lessons to teach my ladies' class. As I began studying these scriptures, I realized this study was exactly what I needed. The words became so comforting. I felt assured in my hopelessness by a peace that surpassed all understanding.

Have you ever opened your Bible to the exact scripture you needed at the time? Write it here:

Explain how the Scriptures are designed to provide exactly what is needed. How can you access this comfort? (Malachi 3:10; Philippians 4:19; 2 Peter 1:3; 2 Timothy 3:16).

One scripture came to me several years before my dad's stroke. I will never forget it. I remember where I was and how I felt when I read it because it gave me a comforting answer to a problem I was facing.

But as for you, you meant evil against me: but God meant it for good, in order to bring it about as it is this day, to save many people alive (Genesis 50:20).

The words of Joseph provided much-needed clarity at that moment. They helped me to understand that everything God is doing is for my good.

As I thought about Joseph and all he endured, I remembered how God used him to save His people. There was purpose in his pain. That is exactly what happened in that hospital room every night as I studied the Twenty-third Psalm. The discoveries within the Psalm never ceased!

As I look back on that time—almost twelve years now—I am awed and amazed at how God carried me through. I believe that with God there are no accidents. Either He is in complete control and knows everything about us or He doesn't. I don't believe in luck or chance when it comes to the Divine.

He is with me every step of every day. He is with me every hour and every minute. He is in every heartbeat and every breath. He is up close and personal, and He knows every one of my difficulties. He also knows yours. He is aware of every tear that slowly falls down my cheek and every tremble of my chin. He is aware of my hurting heart and my feelings of hopelessness. Psalm 56:8 says, "You number my wanderings; put my tears into Your bottle; are they not in Your book?"

What does Psalm 56:8 teach you about the Shepherd who loves you?
Turn our cares over to God.

Read Deuteronomy 31:6 aloud. How does this verse bring you comfort?
It reminds me to be strong, courageous & not be afraid because God is with me & won't leave me.

Our Good Shepherd is always there providing, giving us rest, leading us on the right paths, and going ahead of us to prepare exactly what we need. I learned through my experience that I have a God I can trust, and that my Lord Jesus is always with me. That's the Shepherd I want you to know.

You have taken account of my miseries; put my tears in your bottle. You have recorded each one in your book

THE SHEPHERD'S DAUGHTER

—— *Sheep Homework* ——

The Lord is my shepherd, I shall not want

1. Recite the Twenty-third Psalm.

2. What verse has special meaning for you at this moment?

3. Meditate on Psalm 56:8.

4. Write your response to Matthew 10:30. How does it bring comfort to your heart? *(hairs on head are numbered) God knows me well & He cares deeply for me.*

Many years ago, I came across the following poem which became my go-to when I felt discouraged and needed a lift.

Don't Quit

When things go wrong, as they sometimes will,
When the road you're trudging seems all uphill,
When the funds are low and the debts are high,
And you want to smile, but you have to sigh,
When care is pressing you down a bit—
Rest if you must, but don't you quit.

Life is queer with its twists and turns,
As every one of us sometimes learns,
And many a failure turns about
When he might have won had he stuck it out.
Don't give up though the pace seems slow—
You may succeed with another blow.

Often the goal is nearer than
It seems to a faint and faltering man;
Often the struggler has given up
When he might have captured the victor's cup;
And he learned too late when the night came down,
How close he was to the golden crown.

Success is failure turned inside out—
The silver tint in the clouds of doubt,
And you never can tell how close you are,
It might be near when it seems afar;
So stick to the fight when you're hardest hit—
It's when things seem worst that you must not quit.

—Edgar A. Guest

Say that last line aloud: *It's when things seem worst that you must not quit!* That's what the Twenty-third Psalm came to mean to me: "Don't quit, Debbie! The Good Shepherd is with you, encouraging you, and holding you with His strong right arm. He is for you, not against you."

2 Oh, the Benefits of Being the Shepherd's Daughter

Recite the Twenty-third Psalm.
At the end, add, "Oh, the benefits of being the Shepherd's daughter."

We have all things and abound; not because I have a good store of money in the bank, not because I have skill and wit with which to win my bread, but because the Lord is my Shepherd.

—Charles Haddon Spurgeon

I f we're going to know the Shepherd of the Twenty-third Psalm, we must know the benefits of being under His care. Our Shepherd offers us contentment and fulfillment through every season of our lives, not just when we die. From the moment we become a child of God, He is there overseeing our lives every step of the way, and what a comfort that is.

Notice each verse in the Twenty-third Psalm as I explain its meanings. I want you to see from the beginning of this study the benefits of being the Shepherd's daughter.

- "The Lord is my shepherd": He is my master, leader, and owner, and I must surrender. If He is in control that means I don't have to be.
- "I shall not want": He is my provider, meeting all of my needs.
- "He makes me to lie down in green pastures": He gives me contentment, keeping me from worrying about my future.
- "He leads me beside the still waters": He provides rest and refreshment for my weary soul when I feel overwhelmed and unsure.
- "He restores my soul": He will restore me when I feel defeated and frustrated, or when I have fallen under temptation.
- "He leads me in the paths of righteousness for His name's sake": He keeps me on the move for my good; He already knows where He will lead me. I follow His will because His name is at stake.
- "Yea, though I walk through the valley of the shadow of death, You are with me." Even when the valley gets deeper, He continues to walk with me, eventually leading me to higher ground.
- "Your rod and Your staff, they comfort me": He is there protecting and guiding me. He has all authority in my life.
- "You prepare a table before me in the presence of my enemies": He has already prepared a way for me, and He is well aware of my enemy Satan.
- "You anoint my head with oil": His Spirit is in me and His word helps me cope with all of the agitations and annoyances in my life.

20

- "My cup runs over": He blesses me beyond measure. It is a continuous flow of blessings.

- "Surely goodness and mercy will follow me all the days of my life": No matter where I go, no matter what I do, I can't get away from His goodness and mercy. It follows me wherever I go!

- "And I will dwell in the house of the Lord forever": He is with me now, every minute of every day, and then I will be with Him eternally. He has already provided a home for me in heaven.

Recite the Twenty-third Psalm again, but add these words at the end of the psalm: "Oh, the benefits of being the Shepherd's daughter."

As I mentioned at the beginning of preview 1, it was during those dark lonely nights in the hospital room that I discovered that I have a Good Shepherd that is perfectly able to carry me through any situation. As I write this, my mind is flooded with memories. I remember thinking one night as I studied at the hospital, "Yes, I am my daddy's daughter, but more important, I am the Shepherd's daughter," and that means I am under His watchful eye and care 24/7, 365 days a year, every moment, every day. And so are you.

Sheep Homework

1. Recite the Twenty-third Psalm. After the psalm, repeat: Oh, the benefits of being the Shepherd's daughter!

2. Which verses comfort you most? Record them here.

3. Look back at the explanation of each verse. Explain the benefits of being the Shepherd's daughter. *There are many!*

4. Pray and ask the Lord to help you trust Him with your life.

3 The Background of Psalm 23

The Lord Calls Me a Sheep

Recite the Twenty-third Psalm.

At the end, add, "Oh, the benefits of being the Shepherd's daughter."

Before we delve into the Twenty-third Psalm, I want you to know that I can speak to you as one of the sheep because I have walked with the Lord as a sheep in need of a good shepherd. In addition to God's knowing us, we need to know God and His heart. That knowledge will change our perspective about life.

I've been through many things in my life. I have had joys and regrets. I have been broken and betrayed, as you may have been, and I have shed many tears. But no matter what might have happened to me, I have learned that He has been my Shepherd through all of it, and He is there for you too.

I want you to know the benefits of being the Shepherd's daughter, because they are tremendous. When you come to know Him, that is all you will ever want, because He's all you need.

In his beautiful book, *I Shall Not Want*, Robert T. Ketcham tells of a Sunday school teacher who asked her group of children if anyone could quote the entire Twenty-third Psalm. A golden-haired four-and-a-half-year-old girl was among those who raised their hands. A bit skeptical, the teacher asked if she could really quote the entire psalm.

The little girl came to the front of the room, faced the class, made a perky little bow, and said, "The Lord is my shepherd, that's all I want." She

Cute!

22

bowed again, went back to her seat, and sat down. That may well be the greatest interpretation of the Twenty-third Psalm ever heard.[1]

When you know your Good Shepherd, that is all you will ever want or need!

Background of the Twenty-third Psalm

The Bible was written by humble men guided by the Holy Spirit. Much of its terminology and teaching is couched in rural life. Many of the writers lived a nomadic lifestyle. They were familiar with livestock, crops, the land, and wildlife, a far cry from our hurried, urban, man-made stressful way of life today.

Just think. We are familiar with the fast-paced life. We can send messages through the internet and text one another in mere seconds to anyplace in the world. We can grab a sandwich at a drive-thru and be on our way in a short time. We can press a button on our microwave and—poof!—dinner is served.

How does a fast-paced lifestyle keep us disconnected from God?

There are too many distractions.

The average American is far removed from a farm-like way of life. Perhaps our lack of knowledge of rural life is the reason this particular psalm is so misunderstood. We don't know about the care of sheep, and we certainly don't understand the shepherd's point of view. However, we must keep these facts in mind as we study this psalm to help us understand its meaning and context.

Misunderstanding the Meaning of the Twenty-third Psalm

Outside of John 3:16, the Twenty-third Psalm is the most often quoted and most loved passage in the Bible. That psalm is cited so often at funerals that many have come to believe it is about death and dying; however, that is not the case. It is about the full abundant life of a sheep under the care of the Good Shepherd.

---

1 "Church Humor," Inspire21.com, accessed July 1, 2019. http://inspire21.com/stories/humorstories/ChurchHumor.

Each verse of the psalm gives us a picture of what life becomes with the Shepherd. As I began my study many years ago, my perspective and relationship with the Lord began to change. I came to understand that He wants us to experience a good life here, not just in the hereafter.

Jesus spoke of a full abundant life with Him here and now: "I have come that they may have life, and that they may it more abundantly" (John 10:10).

Why do most people associate Psalm 23 with death? *because of the part that says, "Yea, though I walk through the valley of the shadow of death, you are with me,"*

Why is it hard for us to understand that Jesus came to give us an abundant life upon the earth? *It's not hard for me to understand.*

How does knowing the true meaning of Psalm 23 change your perspective? *It reinforces what I already know & believe in my faith.*

Who Wrote the Twenty-third Psalm?

David, later known as the Shepherd King, penned this masterpiece. He grew up as a shepherd boy, tending his father's flock. He was quite familiar with sheep and shepherding. God sent the prophet Samuel to anoint David as the new king for Israel. When Samuel arrived at Jesse's house to anoint the king of Israel, David was out tending his father's sheep. After Samuel had examined all the other sons, he inquired of Jesse,

> "Are all the young men here?" Then he said, "There remains yet the youngest, and there he is, keeping the sheep." And Samuel said to Jesse, "Send and bring him. For we will not sit down till he comes here." So he sent and brought him in. Now he was ruddy, with bright eyes, and good-looking. And the Lord said, "Arise, anoint him; for this is the one!" (1 Samuel 16:11–12).

Psalm 78:70 tells us that God also chose David His servant "and took him from the sheepfolds."

Who wrote Psalm 78? *Uncertain*

24

78:52 ... he led them like sheep through the wilderness
78:53 ... guided them to safety
78:70-71 ... and David shepherded them

Did the author know something about sheep? Explain your answer.

yes

It has been assumed that David wrote the Twenty-third Psalm later in his life. However, there is no indication given concerning the time or circumstance of writing. Yet, as you read, notice how it's written. It seems to reveal someone who has walked with the Lord a long time. It describes a close-knit relationship, one of utter dependence upon the Shepherd. Note the following facts as you recite Psalm 23:

- The psalm is intensely personal; notice the "He/me" and "I/Lord."
- The psalm is written about one man and his life with God.
- In six short verses, the writer refers to himself seventeen times, and thirteen times he refers to the Lord.

This psalm is written in first person about the shepherd from the sheep's perspective. Listen to what the writer says:

> The Lord is my shepherd; I shall not want. He makes me to lie down in green pastures; He leads me beside the still waters. He restores my soul; He leads me in the paths of righteousness for His name's sake.

Of course, we are the sheep. Can you imagine standing in a lush green pasture and speaking directly to other sheep across the way, describing the excellent care of your Shepherd, boasting and explaining what it is like to belong to the Good Shepherd? Get that picture in your mind.

A Messianic Psalm

Psalm 23 is known as one of the "Messianic Psalms." Psalms 22–24 imply a foreshadowing in the Old Testament to give us a picture of Jesus Christ. David wrote of his own trials and sufferings, while guided by the Holy Spirit. David's descriptions foreshadow in detail many of the circumstances and sufferings of the crucifixion of our Lord Jesus Christ. Each psalm gives a contrasting mural of images concerning our Good Shepherd.

Psalms 22–24 were written to be read all together as one psalm. I suggest you read it this way.

Record Psalm 22:1. Jesus quoted this verse in Matthew 27:46 while He hung on the cross. *My God, my God, why have you forsaken me...?*

Read and compare Psalm 22:14–18 and John 19:23–30. Think about all that Jesus fulfilled as He hung on the cross. Record your thoughts. *poured out like water bones and joint relates heart like wax ... melted crucifixion*

Identifying the Good Shepherd

- "I am the good shepherd. The good shepherd gives His life for the sheep" (John 10:11).

- "I am the good shepherd; and I know My sheep, and am known by My own. As the Father knows Me, even so I know the Father; and I lay down My life for the sheep" (John 10:14–15).

- "I will establish one shepherd over them, and he shall feed them—My servant David. He shall feed them and be their shepherd. And I, the Lord, will be their God, and My servant David a prince among them; I, the Lord, have spoken" (Ezekiel 34:23–24).

Who Is the Good Shepherd of Your Soul?

As the months and years passed during this season of my life, I came to understand that the Good Shepherd of my soul became my sustainer, guide, companion, and encourager. This time in my life became a special walk with Him, as this Shepherd's daughter learned of His gracious goodness.

Jesus / my Heavenly Father

Sheep Homework

1. Recite the Twenty-third Psalm.

2. Repeat these words: "The Twenty-third Psalm is not about death but about an abundant life with the Shepherd."

3. Pray a prayer asking the Lord to help you see Him as He is: up close and personal in your life.

4. Ponder: What do I need to understand about His gracious goodness?

4 I Am a Sheep! Unflattering Facts about Sheep

Recite the Twenty-third Psalm.
At the end, add, "Oh, the benefits of being the Shepherd's daughter."

It's always better to be His sheep than not to be. It's better to be in a mud hut in the middle of a jungle with God than to live in a palace without Him. He never witholds anything good from us when we truly follow Him. Oh, the benefits of being the Shepherd's daughter.

This lesson brings a new perspective for us as sheep under His care. When I say "for us as sheep," we must understand who we are: We are sheep. Let's learn the characteristics of sheep to understand the meaning behind each verse. We are called "sheep" in the Scriptures for a reason. Here's a little secret: It's not flattering to be called a sheep. But once you realize their characteristics, you will completely understand why we, like sheep, need the Good Shepherd.

- Sheep are timid creatures, very stubborn, and one of the dumbest animals on this planet. I read once there are no IQ tests for sheep because they have nothing to test. I know that doesn't sound flattering to the human creation, but it is true when it comes to sheep.

- Sheep are unable to take care of themselves. They require meticulous care, more than any other livestock.

- Sheep cannot be left alone.

- Sheep will not drink from rushing water because they are afraid.

- Sheep are known for their mob instincts. If one sheep decides to jump the fence or go over a cliff, the others will follow. A shepherd wrote of one unruly sheep that jumped across a deep ravine. He lost four hundred sheep because the entire flock followed that stray sheep to their deaths. When a shepherd has a sheep that constantly breaks down fences, wanders from the flock, and will not conform to the Shepherd's rule, the shepherd is left with a hard choice. He usually kills that rogue sheep to protect the others.

- Sheep are easily discontented. Everything must be just right within the flock for the sheep to flourish. They must have adequate food and clean, still water to remain healthy. They must have an acute awareness of their shepherd in order to be contented animals. When the shepherd is near, the sheep feel safe.

- Sheep are easily stressed. The slightest irritation can cause them to become greatly upset.

- Sheep do not like to be alone. If alone, they get lost and will become so stressed that they cannot find their way back to the flock. The stress of it leaves them unable to think rationally.

- Sheep are nervous animals, easily spooked. If a jackrabbit or small mouse runs in among them, they will run for dear life and create a stampede.

- Sheep butt heads with each other and fight amongst themselves.

- Sheep want to be the "top sheep" and do things their own way.
- Sheep must be led.

Humanly and Spiritually Speaking

Compare sheep to human beings. How are we like them?

- Are we stubborn?
- Are we easily stressed?
- Are we afraid and fearful at times?
- Do we have mob instincts and the desire to follow the crowd?
- Do we wander away spiritually from the Lord?
- Do we ever experience discontentment?
- Do we butt heads with people? Do we argue, fuss, fight, and fume?
- Do we have to be "top sheep," always thinking we are right?
- Are we easily led, or do we want to go our own way?
- Do we behave foolishly, refusing to listen and doing senseless things?

What Does the Bible Say about Sheep?

We covered the background of David and the psalm itself. Now let us turn our attention to how, as God's children, we are compared to sheep throughout the Scriptures. Answer the following questions about sheep from the Bible.

 Who are we as His people (Psalm 100:3)?

 When we are distressed and dispirited, how are we described (Matthew 9:36)?

 What do we learn about sheep from Isaiah 53:6? Are we guilty?

29

Explain how Luke 12:32 and Jeremiah 50:6 bring you comfort as you see yourself as one of His sheep. Meditate on the verses and record your thoughts here:

According to Hebrews 13:20, how is the Shepherd identified?

The behavior and attitudes of sheep and humans are frighteningly similar. We must get familiar with sheep, because sheep represent us metaphorically throughout Scripture. To truly understand the psalm, it is essential to see ourselves as sheep.

Some have said: "I do not need a shepherd, because I am not a sheep." I hate to inform them, but we are a pitiful lot without our Good Shepherd to lead us through every season of our lives.

It is no accident that the Lord calls us sheep. When we can grasp this, we can recognize our great need for His guidance. Do you comprehend who you are? If so, just bleat these words: "Baaaaa Baaaaa! I am a sheep!"

Sheep Homework

1. Recite the Twenty-third Psalm.

2. Contemplate your need as a sheep in His care.

3. Identify your "sheep" habits.

4. Record Psalm 100:3. What does this verse teach you about you?

SECTION 2

Sheep to Sheep

What David Says as a Sheep

—— SHEEP TO SHEEP ——

Under
His Watchful Eye

The Lord Is

 Recite the Twenty-third Psalm.
At the end, add, "Oh, the benefits of being the Shepherd's daughter."

A man in a Walmart check-out line began a conversation with one of my Bible-class members. During the conversation she made a reference to the Lord. He asked where she attended worship and after she told him, she proceeded to say, "We are studying the Twenty-third Psalm."

He responded, "Do you know my favorite part of that psalm?"

"No," she said with anticipation in her voice.

He said, "The Lord is."

"Why is that?" she asked.

"Because just knowing that He exists, and that He always has been and always will be brings me such comfort. He is in control and I don't have to be."

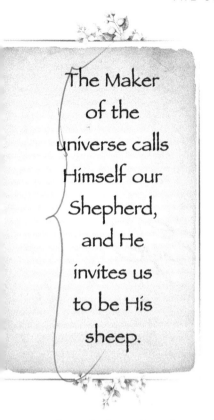

The Maker of the universe calls Himself our Shepherd, and He invites us to be His sheep.

I agree with him. Just knowing "the Lord *is*" is quite enough, but it gets even better. David explains what that means for us as His sheep.

When I look into the night sky and gaze at the vastness of the galaxies, I look toward 250 million times 250 million heavenly bodies that are larger than the sun. They were created and placed in their orbits by the hands of Jesus. It excites me to know that He calls me His. The Maker of the universe calls Himself our Shepherd, and He invites us to be His sheep. Think about that.

He Knows You

Have you ever felt like no one seems to understand your situation or that no one cares about you? Have you said to yourself, "I feel completely alone"? I know at times we have all experienced these feelings, but the good news is that we have a Shepherd who understands everything about us.

- He knows you.
- He knows your story.
- He knows your background and all your family history.
- He knows your strengths and weaknesses.
- He knows your temptations.
- He knows what you need.

He knows every miniscule detail of your life, and He doesn't see us as one big flock of sheep because He knows us individually: by name, personally, and intimately. Isaiah 43:1 says, "I have called you by your name; you are Mine." That's personal.

UNDER HIS WATCHFUL EYE

Our Shepherd is real. He *is*, present tense. Read each of the following verses and record the "benefits."

"I am the good shepherd. The good shepherd gives His life for the sheep" (John 10:11). What does the Good Shepherd do for His sheep? *gives His life*

"I am the good shepherd, and I know My sheep, and am known by My own" (John 10:14). What does the Good Shepherd know about you? *everything*

"My sheep hear My voice, and I know them, and they follow Me" (John 10:27). What should we do as His sheep? What does this verse teach you about Him and knowing your situation? *follow Him*

Do these three verses convey to you that your Shepherd is within your reach? *yes!*

Remember Your Characteristics

As we learned facts about sheep, we also learned that we are like them.

- We are stubborn.
- We like to follow the crowd.
- Sometimes we are stressed, discontent, and nervous.
- We have needs that have to be met physically and spiritually.
- Oh, how we need a Shepherd!

Who is *Yahweh*? *my shepherd*

Notice as the sheep speaks: "Yahweh is my shepherd."

David wrote this as one of the sheep. Picture a little sheep talking to sheep across the road in another pasture: "Look who my shepherd is. The Lord is. He is my owner, my manager." You can almost sense the pride this sheep has in proclaiming to whom he belongs. David used the name that God called Himself: *Yahweh.*

Scripture plainly describes our Lord Jesus as the Shepherd in the verses below.

All of you will be made to stumble because of Me this night, for it is written: "I will strike the Shepherd, and the sheep of the flock will be scattered" (Matthew 26:31).

I am the good shepherd. The good shepherd gives His life for the sheep (John 10:11).

Now may the God of peace who brought up our Lord Jesus from the dead, that great Shepherd of the sheep, through the blood of the everlasting covenant (Hebrews 13:20.)

As Christians, we must realize the significance of who our Shepherd is and the claim that you and I get to make as His sheep.

- Our Shepherd is the all-powerful, all-knowing, all-seeing God of the universe, Jesus Christ.
- Our Shepherd is the God who creates, though He was not created (John 1:1–5, 14–18).
- Our Shepherd is the God who makes and was never made.

The Same as in the Beginning: *Yahweh*

Why is it important to recognize that the Lord *is*? What is the significance of recognizing the Good Shepherd as "the same as in the beginning"? Because we live in a world that is ever changing. But our Lord never changes.

It is indisputable that Jesus is Yahweh.

He is the image of the invisible God, the firstborn over all creation. For by Him all things were created that are in heaven and that are on earth, visible and invisible, whether thrones or dominions or principalities or powers. All things were created through Him and for Him. And He is before all things, and in Him all things consist (Colossians 1:15–17).

In the beginning was the Word, and the Word was with God, and the Word was God. He was in the beginning with God. All things were made through Him, and without Him nothing was made that was made. In Him was life, and the life was the light of men. And the light shines in the darkness, and the darkness did not comprehend it (John 1:1–5).

What does Hebrews 13:8 mean to you?

p 1396   JC is the same yesterday, today & forever!   (He never changes)

The God Who Sees Me: *El Roi*

When Moses was a shepherd, he met God at the burning bush and they had the following conversation:

> Then Moses said to God, "Indeed, *when* I come to the children of Israel and say to them, 'The God of your fathers has sent me to you,' and they say to me, 'What is His name?' what shall I say to them?" And God said to Moses, "I AM WHO I AM." And He said, "Thus you shall say to the children of Israel, 'I AM has sent me to you'" (Exodus 3:13–14).

Our God is Yahweh. He is unchanging, uncaused, ungoverned. Yahweh is our Shepherd. And our Shepherd is *El Roi*, the-God-Who-Sees-Me. Hagar, an Egyptian slave of a Hebrew woman, addressed God as *El Roi*:

> We live in a world that is ever changing. But _our_ Lord never changes.

> Then she called the name of the Lord who spoke to her, You-Are-the-God-Who-Sees; for she said, "Have I also here seen Him who sees me?" (Genesis 16:13).

Describe what it means that your Good Shepherd is *El Roi*; the God-Who-Sees-Me.

That He is omniscient & omnipotent

Yahweh is our Shepherd. He sees us and our needs. To think that David links a lump of clay to Divine destiny! This should stir our hearts to think our

Shepherd is so deeply concerned for us. When I came to this understanding as I studied the psalm, my heart felt as though it was wrapped in a warm blanket. I felt up close and dear to the heart of the God-Who-Sees-Me. What about you? *... have often described this same feeling myself!*

> *God dwells in eternity but time dwells in God. He has already lived all our tomorrows as He has lived all our yesterdays.*
>
> **—A. W. Tozer**

Sheep Homework

1. Rest in the fact that your Good Shepherd is the God-Who-Sees-Me. Study Genesis 16:13.

2. What is your situation? He knows your story, and He sees every detail of your life.

3. Memorize John 10:14. Think upon the fact that you are known by Him.

4. Ask the Good Shepherd to wrap your heart in comfort like a warm blanket and feel His loving presence.

3 I am the Good Shepherd and I know my sheep, and am known by My own

The Names of God in Psalm 23

Verse 1: The LORD is my shepherd; *[Jehovah-Rohi]*
Jehovah-Rohi means "The LORD is my Shepherd."

I shall not want *[Jehovah-Jireh]*
Jehovah-Jireh means "The LORD Will Provide."

Verse 2: He makes me to lie down in green pastures, He leads me beside the still waters *[Jehovah-Shaloam]*
Jehovah-Shaloam means "The LORD of Peace."

Verse 3: He restores my soul *[Jehovah-Rapha]*
Jehovah-Rapha means "The LORD Who Heals."

Verse 4: He leads me in the paths of righteousness for His name's sake *[Jehovah-Tsidkenu]*
Jehovah Tsidkenu means "The LORD Our Righteousness."

Verse 5: You anoint my head with oil *[Jehovah-Mekaddishkem]*
Jehovah-Mekaddishkem means "The LORD Who Satisfies."[2]

Notice the names of God in each verse and their meanings. What does this mean for your life as a Shepherd's daughter?

... that He takes care of me in every way!

---

2 "Names of God," pamphlet, stock #452X (Rose Publishing; 2003).

Claim
Surrender and Ownership

My Shepherd

Recite the Twenty-third Psalm.
At the end, add, "Oh, the benefits of being the Shepherd's daughter."

Shepherds mark their sheep to claim ownership. Many years ago shepherds notched the ears of the sheep to distinguish them from the sheep of nearby shepherds. Should a sheep stray from the flock, the mark on its ear would tell other shepherds to separate that sheep from their flock and return it to the proper owner.

Today shepherds put rings in their sheep's ears or mark them with spray paint.

When the sheep in our passage makes the claim, "The Lord is *my* shepherd," he is saying, "I belong to my shepherd and not another." Expressed in a different way, "He is mine and I am His." After understanding the mark of the shepherd, it is obvious that not all sheep can make that claim.

A seventeenth-century Welch poet said it this way:

> The God of love my Shepherd is,
> And he that doth me feed;
> While he is mine and I am his,
> What can I want or need?

—George Herbert

Who Belongs to the Good Shepherd?

Imagine sheep standing in a barren pasture, under the ownership of an evil sheepman. His stock is thin and weak, riddled with disease and parasites. If his sheep were able to speak, I'm sure they would say, "Oh, how I wish I could make the claim that I belong to the good shepherd across the road. My dreams would be fulfilled if only I could be set free from the ownership of my evil shepherd."

What makes the good shepherd's sheep different? The other sheep don't belong to the good shepherd. They cannot claim ownership because they do not bear his mark.

Read Ezekiel 34:1–10. How does an evil shepherd takes care of his sheep? *He doesn't! He only cares for himself. They scatter & become prey*

Read Ezekiel 34:11–31. Record how many times "my sheep" and "my flock" are used. Write down the benefits of being under the care of the Good Shepherd in this passage. *being protected, safe, well cared for & knowing God* *7 times*

According to Matthew 7:21–23, who enters the kingdom of heaven? What futile claims of ownership did the lawless make? Why were they futile? *he who does the will of the Father who is the k of heaven! the lawless will claim to do things in our Lord's name; futile because they* *p1099* What must a sheep do in order to claim he belongs? *He must follow his shepherd then as they were lawless*

According to Jesus, which way does a sheep enter in with the shepherd (Matthew 7:13–14)? *by the narrow gate*

42

What do these verses teach us about those who claim "the Lord is my shepherd"? *... not to be distracted & led astray onto many path*

We cannot have it both ways. We either belong or we don't. Jesus makes it clear that some will claim to be His when He doesn't know them (Matthew 7:21–23). As His sheep, we are under His authority and direction. It is the Shepherd who guides and directs the sheep, and that means we have to do it His way. Sheep that want to do things their way always end up in trouble.

So many are quick to claim "The Lord is my Shepherd," but do not follow His will or commands. My intention is not to sound harsh or unkind, but I believe that because of our present culture's philosophy of "live and let live," we have forgotten that God has a standard, and He is the only authority.

He tells us what we must do in order to become His sheep. You will find an explanation later in the chapter. Saying "Lord, Lord" doesn't make one His sheep, because Jesus plainly said, "Not everyone who says to Me, 'Lord, Lord,' shall enter the kingdom of heaven, but he who does the will of My Father in heaven" (Matthew 7:21).

> *Jesus makes it clear that some will claim to be His when He doesn't know them.*
>
> **—Matthew 7:21–23**

Mrs. Gadabout

Phillip Keller writes about a ewe called Mrs. Gadabout. He states that she was beautifully proportioned, strong, and had an excellent coat of wool. She bore sturdy lambs that matured rapidly. But despite her wonderful attributes, she was restless, discontented, and a fence crawler. She seemed always to find a hole in the fence, crawl through, and feed on the other side.

She repeatedly left the fold, and she also taught her lambs the same tricks. In a short time, she began to lead other sheep through the same holes and over dangerous paths. She never seemed to understand whose authority she was under. She wanted to do things her way. She could not surrender her own will.

Keller writes that after putting up with her tactics for a period of time, she had to go. Her career of fence crawling was cut short. Mrs. Gadabout became mutton stew. That was the only solution to the dilemma.[3]

The Authority Battle

Why do you think *surrender* is a hard word? Surrender means to cease from resisting and submit to authority. Just as in battle, when we surrender, we raise the white flag. What does it mean to surrender your life totally to the will of the Good Shepherd?

- Does it mean we have to give up our own bad behavior? *Yes*
- Does it mean we have to give up our secret sins? *Yes*
- Does it mean we have to give up our way of thinking improperly? *Yes*
- Does it mean we have to give up our own way of treating others? *Yes*

I read a perfect analogy of my will versus God's will. My life is one of surrender. Surrendering means to search out God's will and follow His plan. If I throw out a boat hook and catch hold of a sapling on the shore and pull, do I pull the shore to me, or do I pull myself to the shore? Surrender is not pulling God to my will but aligning my will to His.

 Ponder and discuss the "boat hook" analogy.

 What do you need to surrender to God's will?

Just as sheep like to go their own way, we do too. A Frank Sinatra classic of yesteryear summarizes how so many people feel today: "I Did It My Way."

---

3 W. Phillip Keller, *A Shepherd Looks at Psalm 23* (Grand Rapids, MI: Zondervan, 1974), 33–34.

But as we saw in the fate of Mrs. Gadabout, our way is not always wise. Sheep that do not surrender don't do well in the flock.

Some Desire Benefits without Membership

In the world of social media, we post our problems or needs on Facebook or Instagram. So many on social media are quick to ask for prayers, and so many want God to show up and bless their lives, yet they aren't part of His flock. They have no intention of submitting to His will. They don't bear His mark of ownership because they are not willing to surrender to Him. Bearing His mark is important, yet our culture wants spirituality without authority.

It is easy to say we are spiritual when we have no intention of submitting to God's authority. We must realize that if we do not bear His mark, we cannot make the claim, "The Lord is *my* Shepherd."

> Surrender is not pulling God to my will but aligning my will to His.

 Discuss and ponder this sentence: "Our culture wants spirituality without submitting to authority."

 How do you think our culture views spirituality?

Bearing the Mark of the Good Shepherd

Now we turn our attention to how we bear the mark of the Good Shepherd. To understand the Bible, we must begin with the basics. There are two laws: The old law (Old Testament) and the new law (New Testament).

As we make application, we must understand that God has always distinguished His sheep from those of other shepherds. He sets His sheep apart, just as any shepherd does.

A study of the old law helps New Testament Christians gain a deeper understanding of what it means to "bear His mark." Under the old law, circumcision became the badge of membership among God's people. It was a distinguishing mark of a Jewish male (Leviticus 12:2–3).

Circumcision, as defined in the Old Testament (Genesis 17), was a symbolic procedure that announced that a Jewish male had entered into a covenant relationship with God.

Now, note a contrast:

> And the LORD your God will circumcise your heart and the heart of your descendants, to love the Lord your God with all your heart and with all your soul, that you may live (Deuteronomy 30:6).

What is mentioned in this passage that gives us a glimpse of a bigger picture? The picture changes in the New Testament. Circumsision, as was practiced under the old law, is no longer required, because we live under a new and better covenant.

> But as it is, Christ has obtained a ministry that is as much more excellent than the old as the covenant he mediates is better, since it is enacted on better promises. For if that first covenant had been faultless, there would have been no occasion to look for a second. For he finds fault with them when he says: "Behold, the days are coming, declares the Lord, when I will establish a new covenant with the house of Israel and with the house of Judah, not like the covenant that I made with their fathers on the day when I took them by the hand to bring them out of the land of Egypt. For they did not continue in my covenant, and so I showed no concern for them, declares the Lord. For this is the covenant that I will make with the house of Israel after those days, declares the Lord: I will put my laws into their minds, and write them on their hearts, and I will be their God, and they shall be my people" (Hebrews 8:6–10 ESV).

According to Colossians 2:11, by whom and through whom are we circumcised today?   _God_

What has been nailed to the cross? (See Colossians 2:11–14 and Romans 8:2.)

Who made it possible for this law to be "wiped out"?

Why was this law nailed to the cross?

According to Colossians 2:11–14, how are we spiritually circumcised today?

What happens when we submit to this spiritual circumcision?

How do we bear the mark of Jesus today?

- We hear about Jesus (Romans 10:17).
- We believe that He is the Son of God (John 3:16).
- We realize our sins and repent (turn away) from those sins (Luke 13:3).
- We confess Jesus before men, and we continue to do so every day of our lives (1 Timothy 6:12; Romans 10:10; 1 John 4:15).
- We are baptized into His death so we can be in the likeness of His resurrection (Romans 6:3–8).

> Bearing His mark is important, yet our culture wants spirituality without authority.

Or do you not know that as many of us as were baptized into Christ Jesus were baptized into His death? Therefore we were buried with Him through baptism into death, that just as Christ was raised from the dead by the glory of the Father, even so we also should walk in newness of life. For if we have been united together in the likeness of His death, certainly we also shall be *in the likeness* of *His* resurrection, knowing this, that our old man was crucified with *Him*, that the body of sin might be done away with, that we should no longer be slaves of sin. For he who has died has been freed from sin. Now if we died with Christ, we believe that we shall also live with Him (Romans 6:3–8).

Answer the following questions based on Romans 6:3–8.

Verse 3: Into whom and into what were you baptized?

Verse 4: What happens when you are baptized?

Verse 5: To whom are you united at this point? (See NASB or ESV.)

Verse 6: What happens to your "old self"?

Verse 7: Explain verse 7 and ponder its meaning.

Verse 8: If you have died with Christ, then what?

Did you get the visual? Baptism is a reenactment of the death, burial, and resurrection of Jesus Christ.

- Just as Jesus died on the cross, we die to our sins.
- After His death, He was buried in a tomb. When we die to our sins, we are buried in water (immersed).

48

- Jesus was raised from the dead and came out of the tomb. When we come up from the water, we are raised as new persons, free from our sins. (See also 2 Corinthians 5:17.)

- Baptism recreates symbolically for us the death, burial, and resurrection of Jesus, and we participate in that. Once we do this, we bear His mark.

What do we do when we are baptized (Galatians 3:27)?

How are we added to the church (Acts 2:47)?

What does Acts 2:38 explain about the forgiveness of sins?

Have you surrendered? Can you make the claim that "He is mine, and I am His"? As the Shepherd's daughter, I raised my white flag a long time ago. I have come to understand that surrender is where the full life begins.

An old hymn expresses it best: "All to thee my blessed Savior, I surrender all." Your Shepherd deserves more than a part-time half-hearted sheep. When you sing that hymn, place extra emphasis on the words *all* and *daily*. And then say this prayer, "Empty me, Lord, so that I can be full of You."

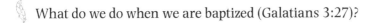

Sheep Homework

1. Meditate upon the Twenty-third Psalm.

2. Be intentional about surrendering your will to God's will.

3. Ask the Lord to help you surrender. Raise your white flag.

4. Sing the hymn "I Surrender All" every day this week.

5. Memorize Galatians 3:27.

Content

As His Sheep

I Shall Not Want

Recite the Twenty-third Psalm.

At the end, add, "Oh, the benefits of being the Shepherd's daughter."

During the years of Dad's illness, every day brought new challenges. I often wondered how the Lord would provide. Thankfully, Dad had saved his money and had a monthly income, but there were many unforseen expenses. The assisted-living home sent a letter telling us they were going up on their monthly fees. Then Dad was rejected by a home health agency due to a technicality. That agency had helped offset many expenses. I felt "panic mode" set in. Little was my understanding at that time—how the Lord always provides.

Throughout the seeming chaos of my life, I picked up on the meaning of contentment. I discerned that "not wanting" was part of being the Shepherd's daughter. God is always going to take care of His children. I learned that

> We must not be half-hearted about our contentment because that says to others, "I lack."

firsthand, as each day my sister and I prayed and trusted the Lord. We became aware, as David did, that if the Lord is your Shepherd, He will take care of you. The time of Dad's illness taught me that there was no need for discontentment. All I needed was to rest in His care and trust His heart.

What Do I Lack?

When David wrote "I shall not want," he comprehended the results of following his Shepherd. He could say "I shall not want" because he could first say "the Lord is my shepherd." David, as the sheep, wants us to believe that "I shall not want" means that he has no reason to worry or fear.

What does "I shall not want" mean? The Hebrew word for "want" means "lack." The Lord is my shepherd; I shall not *lack* anything. For the one who is a follower of the Lord, it means that our fulfillment is found only in God. We may wonder, how can we stop "wanting" for anything. Is it even possible?

The psalm gives us the answer: Our sufficiency is found only in the Lord. It also means that I can live a life of contentment.Because the Lord is my shepherd, my needs will be met, and I can choose to be content with what I have. That means if the Lord is my shepherd and I'm living in this kind of sheep/shepherd relationship with Him, there is no room for complaining.

No Room at the Discontent Inn

Now let's roll up our sleeves and hear the harder lesson. As sheep we must not be half-hearted about our contentment because that says to others, "I lack."

- There is no room for murmuring.
- There is no room for discontentment.

- There is no room for anxiety.
- There is no room for fear or worry.

Most would say, "It's only natural to have these feelings, especially when things go wrong." Is that so? Not if you're living in a contented relationship with your Shepherd. Either "I shall not lack" or "I lack." It cannot be both ways.

Want Versus Need

Let's look a little closer at the promise our Shepherd is making. He promises His sheep the big three: food, shelter, clothing.

I hear you say, "Wait a minute, you just said it means *I will not lack.*" That's true, but we have to understand that it doesn't mean I will have everything I want. It means I will have everything I need.   *Page 1099*

In Matthew 6:25–34 God promises that we do not have to worry about those things because He will always provide our needs. But we must understand there is a big difference in wants and needs. So what is our American standard of needs? How are they different from standards in other cultures?

Here is an example: I may want a cold Dr Pepper and a bag of Cheetos every day, and I don't mean a small bag either. But is that really what I need? No, I really need water and fresh fruit or nuts. And I might want the large bowl of pasta and a basket of garlic bread at the Olive Garden, but I need a salad.

What we often want isn't at all what we need. The idea is to be utterly content in the Shepherd's care. What more should we desire? How does knowing this truth help when it comes to the things we think we need?

> God promises that we are not to worry because He will always provide our needs.

Notice that our Lord supplies our every need, not our every want: "And my God will supply all your need according to His riches in glory by Christ Jesus" (Philippians 4:19).

Take a moment and read Matthew 6:25–34. Notice all of the questions within the text. What does the Good Shepherd want you to learn about worrying? *p 1098-1099*

How does worrying show a lack of faith?
Because our Shepherd provides our needs; as believers we will trust in this

What does Philippians 4:19 promise to provide? *to supply all our needs according to God's riches in glory by Jesus Christ*

Why is it easy for us to believe God's goodness when demonstrated through the lives of God's people found throughout the Bible, but hard to believe it when a great challenge arises in our own life?
... human nature?

How does Psalm 37:25 bring comfort regarding our needs?
p.425 The author is old & hasn't seen the righteous forsaken nor descendants for bread

Think about this: The same one who provided the needs of the children of Israel in the wilderness (Exodus 15–17), the one who sent ravens to feed Elijah by the Brook Cherith (1 Kings 17:1–7), and the one who provided the needs of the disciples He sent out without money or shoes (Luke 22:35) has promised to provide our physical and spiritual needs. We believe their great God made all those provisions, but we have a hard time believing that same God will provide for us.

Remember, our Good Shepherd knows every detail about us. He is always watching us, and He knows what we need before we ask Him (Matthew 6:8).

What do you need? A job? Better finances? Better friends? Someone to love you? We can trust our Good Shepherd when unforeseen circumstances arise. *What if I lose my job?* I shall not want! *What if my health fails me?* I shall not want! *What if the unthinkable happens?* I shall not want!

- God provided the children of Israel all they needed in the wilderness (Exodus 15–17).   *p. 71*

- God sent ravens to feed Elijah by the Brook Cherith (1 Kings 17:1–7).
  p. 396 - 391
- God provided the needs of the disciples when He sent them to preach without money or shoes (Luke 22:35).

p. 11 98

The same One who provided these things for His people will also provide what we need physically and spiritually. We struggle to believe it. However, His promises are true. Believe it!

I have all 3 --- food, clothing, shelter

 Write one of your needs here: _____ .

Now say "I shall not want."

 Why is it so hard for us to understand that God will provide?

Faith don't come in a bushel basket, Missy. It comes one step at a time. Decide to trust Him for one thing today, and before you know it, you find out He's so trustworthy you'll be putting your whole life in His hands.

—Lynn Austin

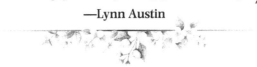

With Your Shepherd, Don't Panic!

In 1 Kings 17:5–6 we read that Elijah "went and did according to the word of the Lord." Elijah traveled to the Brook Cherith that flowed into the Jordan. The ravens kept bringing him bread and meat in the morning and in the evening as God had promised, and he drank from the brook. So if God needs to send "ravens" to feed you in your retirement, He can do it.

Notice 1 Kings 17:7: "And it happened after a while that the brook dried up, because there had been no rain in the land." No more water. It's time to panic. Elijah could have said, *Oh no, Lord, I am in want. How am I going to survive? This nation is under judgment, the brook has dried up, and I don't know what I'm going to do.* But God already knew what He was going to do. (Read 1 Kings 17:10–16.) He sent Elijah to a widow.

If God needs to send a penniless widow to meet the needs of your family, He can do that. We must remember who our Shepherd is. He is Yahweh, the all-powerful, all-knowing, all-seeing God of the universe.

When we find ourselves in need, we must tell ourselves the truth. "I shall not want" is a statement of faith. We can have a conversation with ourselves and remind ourselves that God will provide.

It is important that we learn to counsel our hearts with the truth, to say in any circumstance, "The Lord is my shepherd; I shall not lack what I need." Then we must be content with what God provides. We are safe, and we are secure if the Lord is our Shepherd.

 How would telling yourself the truth about God's care help to comfort you?

I Want What She Has

"I shall not want" is also a statement about self-control. Think about all the pain in life that is caused by *wanting:* "I want this thing." "I want to go to this place." "I want to experience that." "I want to be like her." "I want what they have." Too many of the disappointments of life come from wanting what we do not have. But are we really *lacking?*

One of the most unflattering things about sheep is their discontentment. They become easily upset, even over small things. They want what they want when they want it, and if they don't get it, the scene is not pretty. Let me lovingly remind you: We are sheep.

Listen to these words by fourteen-year-old Jason Lehman:

Present Tense

It was spring, but it was summer I wanted,
The warm days, and the great outdoors.
It was summer. but it was fall I wanted,
The colorful leaves, and the cool, dry air.
It was fall, but it was winter I wanted,
The beautiful snow, and the joy of the holiday season.
It was winter, but it was spring I wanted,
The warmth and the blossoming of nature.
I was a child, but it was adulthood I wanted,
The freedom and the respect.
I was twenty, but it was thirty I wanted,
To be mature and sophisticated.
I was middle aged, but it was twenty I wanted,
The youth and the free spirit.
I was retired, but it was middle age I wanted,
The presence of mind without limitations.
Then my life was over, and I never got what I wanted.

—Jason Lehman[4]

Leads to discontent
What does this poem teach us about "wanting"?
toys *electronics*

Make a list of "wants" according to age groups: (1) children, (2) young
adults, (3) adults with children, (4) mature or elderly. What are the main
sources of discontentment for each age? *more $* *good health*

According to Philippians 4:11–12, what is the solution?

P. 1349 to be content in whatever state I'm in Phil 4:13 I can do all things through Christ who strengthens me!

4 http://www.chicagotribune.com/news/ct-xpm-1989-02-14-8903050524-story.html.

No Good Thing Will He Withhold

Obviously, God wants us to be a happy satisfied people. We shouldn't be restless and jealous, always complaining and ready to panic about what we don't have. We should have a spirit of thankfulness within us that identifies us as belonging to Him.

How should we control ourselves in the presence of others when we are unhappy about certain situations?

Don't complain or panic

What kind of attitude should we display if we are content with our Shepherd? *exhibit a spirit of thankfulness (& praise)*

How does discontentment among Christians hurt our influence? *Who wants to be around someone who constantly exhibits discontent?*

Contentment is the hallmark of the woman who puts her affairs in the hands of God. Contentment is one of the characteristics of the Shepherd's daughter. The Good Shepherd always knows exactly what is best for us and exactly what we need.

> For a day in Your courts is better than a thousand. I would rather be a doorkeeper in the house of my God than dwell in the tents of wickedness. For the Lord God is a sun and shield; the Lord will give grace and glory; no good thing will He withhold from those who walk uprightly (Psalm 84:10-11).

Oh, the benefits of being the Shepherd's daughter!

Sheep Homework

1. Recite the Twenty-third Psalm.

2. Memorize Philippians 4:11–12.

3. Identify discontentment in your own life and pray about it.

4. This week learn to say: "I shall not lack what I need because I can trust my Shepherd!"

How to Be a Contented Sheep

- Stop wanting more.
- Be grateful for what you do have. "Count your blessings."
- Stop complaining. Complaining is like a contagious infection, like a fire that spreads. Children are taught in school: *Stop, Drop, and Roll!* When a negative thought starts, drop it and roll quickly away from the complainer and toward the positive.
- Change your perspective by changing the way you think (Proverbs 23:7). *p 730 For as he thinks in his heart, so is he, "Eat and drink," he says to you but his heart is not with you.*
- Don't compare your life to or mimic someone else. Theodore Roosevelt said, "Comparison is the thief of joy."
- Put people before things; don't allow perfectionism and expectations to keep you away from people.
- Focus on today, one day at a time. "Do not worry about tomorrow, for tomorrow will worry about its own things" (Matthew 6:34).
- Savor the little things.
- Don't wait until everything is perfect before you decide to enjoy your life.
- Once you need less, you'll have more.

2) *Phil 4: 11-12*
"Not that I speak in regard to need, for I have learned in whatever state I am in, to be content,
12. I know how to be abased, and I know how to abound.
Everywhere and in all things I have learned both to be full and to be hungry, both to abound and to suffer need.

Need to
be
free of fear

Free from friction
within the flock
Free of pests
Free of hunger

4

Resting
In His Care

In Green Pastures

Recite the Twenty-third Psalm.

At the end, add, "Oh, the benefits of being the Shepherd's daughter."

← p. 9

The more you read the Bible, the more you'll love the author.

—**Author Unknown**

David becomes an artist in verse 2 as he paints a beautiful word picture of sheep lying down on green grass. Can you see the sheep with their legs folded underneath them, resting in complete contentment while the shepherd stands beside them?

Nearby is a still quiet brook. All is serene, just like a peaceful Sunday afternoon nap. Don't you get a little sleepy just thinking about that? The idea of sheep lying down in a verdant pasture gives us a picture of serenity.

By now I'm sure you have realized that sheep are complicated little animals. For sheep to lie down and rest, certain conditions must be met.

The four basic needs of sheep are that they be:

- Free of fear.
- Free of friction within the flock—no fighting or butting heads.
- Free of pests; no flies allowed.
- Free of hunger.

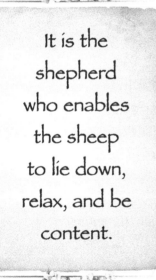

> It is the shepherd who enables the sheep to lie down, relax, and be content.

The shepherd is mindful of each need, and his role is vitally important.

He works to provide lush green pastures for his sheep.

In Palestine, green pastures are not a natural occurrence. The climate is dry and hot, so the land is sun-parched. For the sheep to enjoy the beautiful green pastures amid brown barren hills, the shepherd has to work at planting, fertilizing, and eliminating hindrances such as roots, rocks, and stony ground.

It is the shepherd who enables the sheep to lie down, relax, and be content. The very presence of the shepherd, their master and protector, puts the sheep at ease. He is the only one who completely grasps what they need in order to thrive. The shepherd is keenly aware that when his sheep are well fed and secure, they will lie down to rest.

Free of Fear

The slightest suspicion of danger from predators—dogs, coyotes, cougars, bears—will cause the sheep to rise frightened, ready to run for their lives. They have no means of defense, no sharp claws or fangs to use for fighting. Their legs are too short to escape their natural predators. Sheep are so fearful that even if a tiny mouse were to run amongst them, they would scatter in terror.

Oh, how I can relate to these pitiful sheep. So many times in my life the fear of the unknown or the fear of looming circumstances made it impossible for me to rest.

Can you recall a time when you were fearful? Could you rest? Remember this: "For God has not given us a spirit of fear, but of power and of love and of a sound mind" (2 Timothy 1:7). A sound mind is at peace, at ease, and not disturbed or harassed about the future.

What has God given us to help us overcome fear? *His spirit/ ... of power, love & sound mind*

How can the presence of the Shepherd help you when you are fearful? *He puts us at peace, at ease, & not disturbed or harassed about the future*

How can the definition of "a sound mind" help you when you are struggling to rest? *When we think clearly, we rest in God's promises*

Free of Friction within the Flock

In every animal society there is a pecking order. There are standoffs among any given group of animals. Sheep have the "butting order." Usually it's an old ewe that wants to be the boss.

Philip Keller described how he often watched an austere old ewe walk up to a younger one that might be feeding contentedly or resting quietly in some sheltered spot and begin to butt heads with that sheep. Move over! Out of my way! The rivalry and jealousy over certain spots or feeding grounds turned into a standoff, and sometimes it wasn't pretty.

> *For God has
> not given us a
> spirit of fear;
> but of power,
> and of love
> and of a sound
> [disciplined]
> mind.*
>
> —2 Timothy 1:7

When such conduct becomes common within a flock, the other sheep become edgy, tense, discontented, and restless. They lose weight and become irritable. Are you starting to see a picture of the "human animal"? Doesn't that describe our struggles within our own relationships—family squabbles, marital disagreements, church bickering? Someone always wants to be "top sheep."

We hear of robberies, assaults, wars, fussing, and fighting among people every day. Most news anchors begin the evening news with, "Good evening," and then proceed to tell us what's not good about it.

Why do we have fights, wars, and problems with people butting heads? Because there will always be jealousy, pride, and the feeling that someone has cheated us out of something we deserve! Bottom line: All of the fighting and contention in relationships leave us feeling stressed and uneasy, and we cannot rest. Are you beginning to see why we are called sheep?

What is the source of quarrels and conflicts among you? Is not the source your pleasures that wage war in your members? You lust and do not have; so you commit murder. You are envious and cannot obtain; so you fight and quarrel (James 4:1–2 NASB).

How does James 4:1–2 explain our "top sheep" mentality?

*Desires for pleasures war among
people*

Explain why fighting and quarreling among people cause unrest.

It's unpleasant & there's dissatisfaction

Contrast that conflict with God's people lying down in contentment and peace. The mere presence of the shepherd can create a sense of trust and peace among the flock. All he has to do is appear and the sheep will settle down.

From a spiritual perspective, do we comprehend how "wanting my way" can cause problems?

What would happen in our relationships if we were acutely aware of the presence of our Good Shepherd, Jesus Christ? *Peace, harmony & love!*

What would change if we kept our eyes on the Master and not on those around us? *a better world!*

Put aside bad qualities & be kind & forgiving p 13 40

From the following verses, make a list about our conduct: Ephesians 4:31–32; Colossians 3:13; Matthew 5:9; 7:5; Romans 12:17–19.

p 1353 *bear with P.1096 one another ... bl are plenk from & forgive peacemaker eye P.1293 look for good & live peacably leave vengeance to the Lord feed enemy & give him drink*

Another requirement, free of flies, will be explained in detail in a future chapter. Now we turn our attention to the condition of hunger among the flock.

Free of Hunger

Why does the shepherd need to lead his sheep to the green pastures he provides?

- Hungry ill-fed sheep will not rest!

- Hungry sheep are in constant anguish, causing them to stand on their feet and fret.

- Hungry sheep are never content and will not thrive.

- Malnourished sheep become sick and weak.

Why do sheep need green pastures?

- Lush green grass helps the sheep to grow and flourish.

- Green pastures help to keep the sheep healthy and strong.

- Ewes about to give birth and those that have given birth need heavy milk flow for the baby lambs.

- Baby lambs can gain a hundred pounds within a hundred days after birth, if they have the right pasture.

- Green pastures help the sheep to ruminate, that is, to chew the cud repeatedly for a period of time. *Rumen* is the Latin name for the first stomach compartment of ruminant animals.

- When the sheep are full and able to lie down, rest and rumination are complete bliss for them and the shepherd.

Name the four factors that prevent sheep from lying down to rest.

Why are green pastures so important for the sheep's survival?

How can you accomplish spiritual ruminating?

What does Jesus tell us about those who are blessed in Matthew 5:6?

How is spiritual hunger satisfied? How vital is it for us to nourish ourselves in the green pastures of God's Word? Note these verses: Hebrews 4:12; Joshua 1:8; Psalm 119:11.

Can a lack of spiritual nourishment cause inability to rest? Why or why not?

Sheep won't lie down if they are hungry. What spiritual conclusion can you make for your own life from that statement?

Milk and Honey

It is no accident that the Scriptures call the promised land "a land flowing with milk and honey." In scientific terms "milk flow" and "honey flow" refer to the peak season in the spring and summer when the pastures are the most productive. When the livestock feed on the forage and the bees visit the blossoms, it produces a corresponding flow of milk and honey.

When we visualize the children of Israel moving from Egypt to the promised land, we see a true picture of moving from sin to a place of victory. What about you? Do you need to search for and move into a place of victory? Do you need to be in a land flowing with milk and honey?

Think deeper with me. The green pastures our Shepherd provides are where we find the answers to life's dilemmas and where our needs are met. There we can graze until our heart is content in the green pastures of God's Word.

Let me tell you, it is lush. It is nutrient-filled, and there are no stones or roots to get in our way. Only truth, hope, peace, and forgiveness are offered in this pasture. When we allow the Word of God to lead us and guide us, we are filled with His goodness and mercy. Then we can lie down and rest.

I remember being so overwhelmed with my dad's situation that I couldn't sleep. His health seemed always to be on a roller coaster. I often got calls in the night telling me that Dad was headed to the hospital in an ambulance. It was a time of uncertainty. During those times I needed rest, peace, and assurance, and I always found consolation in the green pasture when I reached for my Bible and started reading, filling my heart with its great truths. Before long I'd be asleep, asleep in the green pasture with my Shepherd. Full. Relaxed and able to rest. I often awoke holding onto my Bible, like Linus to his blanket.

So many times during my season of unrest and uncertainty, I clung to my Bible instead of turning on the television. I realized this wasn't a time for junk food or pastures of wasteland. I needed a transfusion. I needed straight B12 from the pasture of God's Word, and I received it every time. Yes, *He makes me to lie down in green pastures.* What about you?

Share Your Treasure

Sometimes I think we don't make the connection to the nourishment available from the Scriptures. People in other countries value it and treat it as a lifegiving source for their souls.

I am reminded of a story about a missionary in Africa who gave a Bible to a native. Upon receiving it, the man hugged it close and expressed a great appreciation for the precious gift.

But when the missionary saw him a few days later he noticed, much to his dismay, that the Bible looked like it had fallen apart. Many of the pages were missing. The missionary asked him, "What happened? What did you do to your new Bible? When I gave it to you, I thought you considered it a treasured possession."

The man replied, "Indeed, it is very precious. It is the finest gift I have ever received. It is so precious that when I returned to my village, I very carefully chose a page and tore it out to give to my mother. Then I tore out another page and gave it to my father. And I tore out a page and gave it to my wife. Finally, I gave a page of God's Word to everybody who lives in my village."

You may be smiling at this beautiful story, but isn't it a lesson for us that God's Word was such a treasure to him that he wanted to share it with others?

When the Word is our treasure, that is where our hearts will be. Our knowledge of the Word is a mark of true discipleship.

Sheep Homework

1. Recite the Twenty-third Psalm.

2. Use the following scriptures to answer this question: How should we feel about Bible study?

   So Jesus was saying to those Jews who had believed Him, "If you continue in My word, then you are truly disciples of Mine; and you will know the truth, and the truth will make you free" (John 8:31–32 NASB).

   Be diligent to present yourself approved to God, a worker who does not need to be ashamed, rightly dividing the word of truth (2 Timothy 2:15).

3. When Jesus was in the wilderness being tempted by Satan, He was hungry from forty days of fasting. When Satan tempted Him to turn stones into bread, Jesus answered him, saying, "It is written, 'Man shall not live by bread alone, but by every word of God'" (Luke 4:4). What word in Luke 4:4 gives us the impression that God's Word is vital to our spiritual well-being? According to Jesus, what are we to feed on? *The Word!*

4. Be intentional about spending time in the green pastures of God's Word every day.

5. Think of God's Word as your "green pasture."

6. Put together a basket or book bag with your Bible, a notebook or journal, and a pen. Keep it in a designated place so it's handy.

7. Set a time of the day when you can feed in the green pasture. Then "ruminate" in the following hours.

8. What can you share to help someone realize the essentiality of God's Word?

Green Pastures

Sometimes things happen in our lives
Over which we have no control.
Things that cause worry and pain;
Things that defeat our plans and goal.

We seldom find the real answer
Until our hearts cry out to God,
What did I do to deserve this?
Why is life so roughshod?

When we believe in Jesus
And know the battle that He won,
We have hope in our sorrow,
As we grow to love God's Holy Son.

And as we start to trust Him,
We forgive like we are supposed to do,
And we learn to love again,
As we inch our problems through.

God provides the green pastures
And lights our dark valleys too,
And we walk beside still waters,
Which changes our former view.

We start remembering little things
While we traveled in the dark;
The fragrance of Nature's bouquet,
The trees and flowers in the park.

He gave us little gifts along the way
And told us to stop awhile and rest;
And as we listened and obeyed,
We were truly blessed.

And as we looked behind us,
God's love was unveiled;
Now we are looking forward
To eternity's precious, sunny vale.[5]

—Eva May Young

5 http://www.skywriting.net/inspirational/poems/green_pastures.html.

Led
By the Shepherd
Beside Still Waters

Recite the Twenty-third Psalm.
At the end, add, "Oh, the benefits of being the Shepherd's daughter."

We live in a country that praises a fast-paced lifestyle. It seems that we feel more important if we can spout off our "to do" list to someone: "I'm taking care of my sick parent, running to ball practice, taking the kids to piano lessons. Oh, and we have a birthday party at five, and we don't have a gift!"

I remember during the three-and-a-half years of taking care of Dad, I was part of the "sandwich generation," raising an eleven-year-old and a teenager, while caring for my aging parent. I was like that piece of ham in the middle of a sandwich. Life was so busy for me then, and looking back on it now, I really can't explain how I managed it all, except for the Lord's help.

> The shepherd keeps them free from fear, friction, pests, and hunger so they will lie down.

There were days when I felt like the hamster on a wheel, running and running but going nowhere. Even worse, sometimes my hamster left the wheel altogether. A poor little hamster swung off the wheel, lying feet up on the floor. You may chuckle at this image, but every time that happened, my body physically shut me down and I had to go to bed. I lived in the land of overload. We are overloaded with busyness, activities, information, and stress.

Unhealthy Overload

I learned from reading *Overload Syndrome* by Richard A. Swenson that even the best crew in the world can't fix a race car when it's going two hundred miles an hour! What causes you to live in the land of overload? Why can't a race team fix a car while it's going two hundred miles per hour? We know the obvious answer.

Stress happens when we take on too many things, and the pressures of life can cause us to become agitated, overwhelmed, and anxious. To put it simply, we need to stop doing and be; we need to rest.

Still Waters

In the last chapter we discussed the physical and emotional needs that must be met in order for the sheep to rest. The shepherd keeps them free from fear, friction, pests, and hunger so they will lie down.

However, in order for the sheep to flourish, a good shepherd leads them to cool, still waters for a drink. The flock will not drink from water that is moving too fast because they are afraid. Those little stubborn creatures will either thirst to death or drink from mud holes teeming with parasites before they drink from swiftly moving water.

Sheep must have plenty of water in order to ruminate and digest the green grass. Not only do they need clear still water, but they must have it often. Sheep will dehydrate very quickly without a proper water supply.

David, the author of Psalm 23, understood that sheep needed three different sources for water:

1. Dew on the grass: Sheep get up before dawn when the grass has the most dew. As they feed, they drink.

2. Watering holes that the shepherd has provided: That is still water, clean and pest free.

3. Springs or streams that are slow and serene.

What do you picture when you hear the term *still waters?* It simply means restful waters! Have you ever had a day when nothing went right, nothing worked? Your nerves were on edge and you wanted to cry or maybe even scream. Have you ever just needed some peace and rest in your life? If you answered, yes, then you are need of restful waters with your Good Shepherd.

Not from the Mouth of a Child

We realize that most children are free from worry but what if your ten-year-old refused to eat and then remained awake all night? What would she say if you asked, "Honey, what is wrong with you?" I'm sure it wouldn't be, "Mom, I'm worrying about my pension plan."

What if your four-year-old cried out at night and you ran into her room and asked, "Sweet girl, why are you crying?" And she replied, "What if I never pass college chemistry? What if I don't get my driver's license when I'm sixteen?"

Or what if your eight-year-old said, "I'm upset because I'm afraid I'll be a rotten parent." You would probably want to call in a child psychologist. Fortunately, kids don't have such thoughts.

So why is it that we as adults can't seem to find the balance when it comes to rest? We have sacks of burdens and suitcases of worries, and all while we are living fast-paced lives.

What does the Good Shepherd tell us to do when we feel burdened or weary?

> Come to Me, all you who labor and are heavy laden, and I will give you rest. Take My yoke upon you and learn from Me, for I am gentle and lowly in heart, and you will find rest for your souls. For My yoke is easy and my burden is light (Matthew 11:28–30).

The Yoke of Jesus: His Teaching

A yoke for draft animals consisted of a horizontal bar that rested on the animals' necks. Two U-shaped neck braces called *bows* dropped down from the bar and encircled the necks of the animals so they could pull a load together. Yokes, both double and single, were common in Bible times.

Yoke, as generally used in Scripture, refers to an undesired burden, possibly troublesome laws imposed by the Mosaic law, and therefore the word *yoke* "is so transferred to the commands of Christ as to contrast them with the commands of the Pharisees, which were a veritable yoke." Jesus explained that when we accept His yoke—His teaching—He makes the load easy to pull.

Burden holds a similar meaning of the obligation or law that Christ lays on His followers. Although Christ expects obedience, His teachings are light in comparison to those of Moses.

Think about what Jesus said, and substitute the word *teaching* for "yoke" and *law* for "burden."

"Take my *teaching* upon you, and learn from Me. My *teaching* is easy, and My *law* is light."

We will receive His rest if we come to Him and learn from Him. Our load is light when we practice what He teaches us. That's a promise.

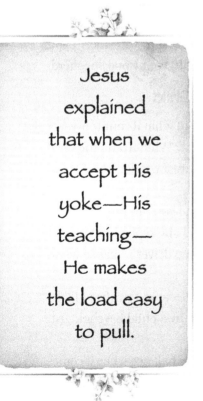

Jesus explained that when we accept His yoke—His teaching—He makes the load easy to pull.

Stop Doing and Be

God is our source of strength. The Lord is with us in chaos, in troubles, and in all the areas that make us afraid. Psalm 46 speaks of a spiritual river, one that flows from the dwelling of the Most High God. Stillness and rest go hand in hand. Our battles cannot be won without the Good Shepherd.

"Be still, and know that I am God" (Psalm 46:10). How do we find rest, according to this verse, and why does that work? "Be still" literally means to stop our frantic activity; to let down. Why is it so difficult for us to stop our frantic activities?

As sheep following our Shepherd, we need to stop in the midst of the pain and chaos and take time to be with Him. Stop doing and *be*. Sometimes the holiest thing we can do is turn off the noise. We need to stop and let Him fill our souls with the serene waters of peace.

 Read Psalm 46. Circle and meditate on the comforting words. Memorize verse 10. Why are we given that command?

Drinking from My Own Cistern

I remember a day when what I had to offer wasn't enough. Dad had become difficult to reason with and my nerves were on edge. Oh, how I needed a day of rest. I just needed to be still and quiet. At one point, most of the responsibility had fallen to me because of some unforeseen circumstances in my sister's family. She was still involved, but temporarily unable to do the things she once did.

To make sure Dad had what he needed, I stayed in contact with the workers at the assisted living home. I visited him several times a week. When I had to miss a regular visit, I called him. Anna, our youngest daughter, was always by my side. She helped and encouraged me during these critical times.

Dad often became angry because he couldn't go home. He became more difficult and started to behave in ways that were not in line with the policies of the assisted living home.

77

One day I got a call: "You've got to come and talk to your dad, or we're going to ask him to leave." The caregiver proceeded to explain that dad was being defiant and would not co-operate with them. She also told me that Dad refused to go to the dining room to eat. He wouldn't take a bath, and he gave them difficulty when taking his medications.

I tried to talk to him, reason with him, and console him, but he just got angrier because he couldn't take care of himself. The reality of his failing body hit him hard, and my heart broke for him. I felt helpless and frustrated.

On one particular visit when Anna and I returned to the car, I said, "Anna, just sit here a minute and let me call Cindy."

"Cindy, what are you doing?" I asked.

"I'm pumping gas," she replied.

"Hold the phone out from your ear," I said.

"Why?" she asked.

I said, "Just do it!" Then I screamed, "Eeeyyaaauuugghhhhh!"

"Are you having a bad day?" she asked.

"What makes you think that? I must have given you the wrong impression."

We laugh about it now, but then it wasn't funny. In fact, it was nerve-racking. Due to circumstances beyond my control, I turned to my own well for a drink. I am human, and my feelings were frazzled.

Sometimes, instead of turning to the Lord, we turn to our own ways to find what we need. God's Word encourages, "The Lord is with you, O valiant warrior" (Judges 6:12 NASB). In complete contrast to Gideon's weakness, God saw something entirely different. No matter the task God puts before us, we need to remember it is not our inability but God's ability.

What happens when we turn to our own wells of water, spiritually speaking?

For my people have committed two evils: They have forsaken Me, the fountain of living waters, and hewn themselves cisterns—broken cisterns that can hold no water (Jeremiah 2:13).

Just as the sheep that search for their own water to satisfy their thirst end up getting sick with liver flukes and parasites, I have gone in search of the wrong water many times. What about you?

Searching for Spiritual Water

What types of "water" do humans in need of rest seek, especially when we are frazzled by life's circumstances? My paraphrase of Jeremiah 2:13 is: "God knows we cannot dig our own well to satisfy ourselves, because our cisterns have cracks. We will not rest or become truly satisfied until we come to Him." We must get it in our minds: He is our source of "still waters."

In John 4, Jesus made an analogy between physical water and spiritual water. As He spoke to a woman who had not been drinking from a spiritual well, He explained the source of still, restful, life-giving water. He also explained that physical waters do not satisfy spiritual thirst and will not give us rest.

We live in a world where people are always looking to anything that will help them rest: drugs, alcohol, addictions, retail therapy that leaves us in debt, sex addictions, and pornography. We want to numb our pain with everything except the one who can satisfy us—Jesus.

> Jesus answered and said to her, "Whoever drinks of this water will thirst again, but whoever drinks of the water that I shall give him will never thirst. But the water that I shall give him will become in him a fountain of water springing up into everlasting life" (John 4:13–14).

 What kind of water does Jesus describe?

 What does He want us to understand, as His sheep?

No matter the task God puts before us remember that it is not our inability but God's ability.

Who is the "Fountain of Living Water"?

Jesus clearly teaches us to rest, and rest must be intentional.

- Mark 6:31—"Come aside by yourselves to a deserted place and rest a while."
- Luke 4:42—"He departed and went into a deserted place."
- Luke 5:16—"So He Himself often withdrew into the wilderness and prayed."

Jesus healed the sick, taught audiences large and small, and performed miracles. He was busy from daylight till dark. However, He always spent time with His Father. So Jesus teaches us, by example, the importance of rest.

 Why must we be intentional when it comes to rest?

"We are His people, and the sheep of His pasture" (Psalm 100:3).

We can feel secure when we rest in Him. Linus, in the *Peanuts* cartoon series, always carried his blanket for security. In one cartoon, Linus said, "My life is full of fear and anxiety. The only thing that keeps me going is this blanket; I need help!" Linus never truly felt secure. But as Jesus' sheep we can be secure, and that means we can rest. "I will both lie down in peace, and sleep; You alone, O Lord, make me dwell in safety" (Psalm 4:8).

Lord is sometimes in all capital letters in the Bible. The anglicized form of that capitalized Lord is *Yahweh,* which refers to the all-knowing, all-seeing, ever-present God of the universe, the one who can hold 340 quintillion gallons of water in His hand! David is describing a sense of security with Yahweh when he says, "You alone, O Lord, make me dwell in safety." We need to memorize Psalm 4:8 and repeat it often. That's rest! That's security!

So go ahead, get out your blanket like Linus, and take a snooze by the still waters. You can rest because He always has one eye open.

Be still, my nerves, and know God's relaxation;
Be still, my heart, and know God's quietness;
Be still, my body, and know God's renewal;
Be still, my mind, and know God's peace.

1. Read Psalm 46 and record the source of your peace.

2. Record the promises.

3. Identify your own "cisterns" that may be the wrong sources of rest and comfort, not from the Shepherd.

4. Be intentional this week as you spend time alone with the Good Shepherd at the still waters of rest.

One night I sat in the dark with my Bible and the book, *A Shepherd Looks at Psalm 23*. As I read the following words, tears streamed down my face.

> Then in the midst of our misfortunes there suddenly comes the awareness that He, the Christ, the Good Shepherd is there. It makes all the difference. His presence in the picture throws a different light on the whole scene. Suddenly things are not so terrifying. The outlook changes and there is hope. I find myself delivered from fear. Rest returns and I can relax.
>
> This has come to me again and again as I grow older. It is the knowledge that my Master, my Friend, my Owner has things under control even when they may appear calamitous. This gives me great consolation, repose and rest. "Now I lay me down in peace and sleep, for Thou God keepest me."[6]

I began to feel joy and unexplainable confidence. Then I started to realize: My Shepherd is nearby, He is watching over me, and He is in this with me. A whole new perspective came to my situation. Suddenly my outlook changed, and my circumstances were not as dreary as they seemed. Hope appeared in the form of the assurance that I am not alone.

---

6 Keller, *A Shepherd Looks at Psalm 23*, 26-27.

6

Belly Up
Restores My Soul

Recite the Twenty-third Psalm.
At the end, add, "Oh, the benefits of being the Shepherd's daughter."

My Great-Aunt's Wardrobe

When my Great-Aunt Alpha passed away, I inherited an antique wardrobe from her estate. The back of one mirror on this historical piece boasts the date: 1864.

The wardrobe was in my mom's storage building for quite a while. When she moved to a new house, she declared, "It's time to claim your wardrobe." I immediately arranged a rescue.

The wardrobe had lost its luster. The mirrors were cracked and discolored, and the hardware was corroded. I'm sure if this heirloom could talk, it would have many stories to tell, because it had survived 153 years.

I selected someone to restore the wardrobe. Three months later, the artisan notified me that it was ready to pick up.

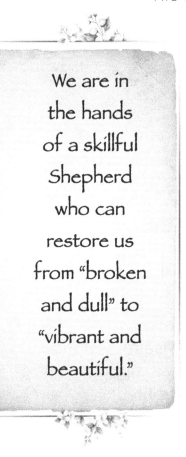

We are in the hands of a skillful Shepherd who can restore us from "broken and dull" to "vibrant and beautiful."

The "before" and "after" pictures are amazing. That heirloom went from sad, broken, and dull to vibrant and beautiful. The hands of an artisan made all the difference.

That's what it is like for us, the sheep in His pasture. We are in the hands of a skillful Shepherd who can restore us from "broken and dull" to "vibrant and beautiful."

When the sheep proclaims, "He restores my soul," the literal translation is, "He causes my life to return to me." The word *restore* in *Webster's Dictionary* means "to replenish" and "to return to its original state, turn back, rescue, to refresh."

Cast Down or Belly Up?

When David said "He restores my soul," the idea was the rescue of a sheep in danger, or a cast-down sheep lying on its back, feet kicking in the air.

Author Phillip Keller writes:

A "cast" sheep is a very pathetic sight. Lying on its back, its feet in the air, it flays away, frantically struggling to stand up, without success. Sometimes it will bleat a little for help, but generally it lies there lashing about in frightened frustration. If the owner does not arrive on the scene within a reasonably short time, the sheep will die. This is why it is so essential for a careful sheepman to look over his flock every day, counting them to see that all are able to be up and on their feet. If one or two are missing, often the first thought to flash into his mind is, "One of my sheep is cast somewhere. I must go in search and set it on its feet again."[7]

---

7 Ibid., 60.

84

I am reminded of the older folks in the TV "Life Alert" commercials. When they fall in the bathtub or out on the golf course, they press their life-alert button and scream: "Help, I've fallen and I can't get up!" That's what it's like for a sheep that has fallen. It cannot get up on its own.

Have you ever been "belly up" and needed restoration? Most of us have. We can feel "cast down" and burdened by physical challenges, emotional pain, and mental exhaustion. Like sheep, we need restoration.

David knew what it meant to be cast down and defeated.

> Why are you cast down, O my soul? And why are you disquieted within me? Hope in God; for I shall yet praise Him, the help of my countenance and my God (Psalm 42:11).

 What feelings or emotions is David describing in this verse?

 What solution does David give for these feelings?

The good news is, our Shepherd is always watching and is ready to stand us on our feet.

Three Reasons Sheep Become "Cast Down"

- *Gases in the rumen:* After eating and drinking, a sheep finds a comfortable spot such as a hollow or a low place to lie down. Gases start to build up in the rumen. The body weight shifts. The sheep rolls over, feet in the air. Blood flow is cut off, especially in the legs.

 How do certain shifts in life leave us feeling "cast down"?

 When do you feel like your circulation has been cut off spiritually?

- *Long heavy fleece:* Sheep can become burdened because of too much wool. The wool becomes matted, muddy, and filled with burrs and manure, making it easy for the sheep to become "cast down." The remedy is for the shepherd to sheer the sheep and get rid of the heavy weight of the wool.

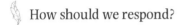 What causes us to become "cast down" by certain weights in our own lives? Sin? Conflicts? Depression? Loss?

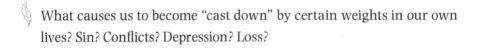 How should we respond?

- *Sheep are overweight:* The shepherd will take steps to correct the weight problem. He puts his flock on a special diet and rations their grain. Every good shepherd wants the flock to be energetic, healthy, and strong.

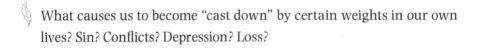 What weights are you carrying that are causing you to feel "cast down"?

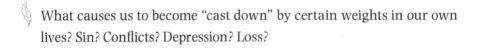 No matter what has caused the sheep to become "cast down," what must be done to save its life?

Adversary on the Prowl for the Cast Down

Not only does the shepherd keep a close watch over the sheep, but so do predators. Wolves, bears, cougars, coyotes, and vultures watch when a sheep is cast down, because they are easy prey. A cast-down sheep has no choice but to lie where he is and be devoured.

Apply the "cast-down sheep" principle to God's children. We have a spiritual enemy—Satan. He is waiting for us to become cast down. Why? Because when we are cast down, we are like a sheep on its back—easy prey. Peter says, "Be sober, be vigilant; because your adversary the devil walks about like a roaring lion, seeking whom he may devour" (1 Peter 5:8).

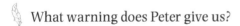 What warning does Peter give us?

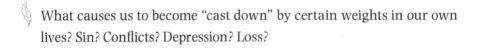 How can his words alert us when we are "cast down"?

The word *devour* in the Greek is *katapien,* meaning "to swallow or to drown." The devil is the real enemy of the Christian, and he is not above using whomever and whatever he can to harm us. His agenda is far beyond physical harm. He wants to destroy us spiritually. Jesus said, "The thief does not come except to steal, and to kill, and to destroy" (John 10:10).

Let me also remind you, dear little sheep, that the enemy wants to steal your joy, kill your zeal and enthusiasm for the Lord, and destroy you spiritually. If he can get us to go belly up, he will move in. Beware! Remember, your battle is not with flesh and blood (Ephesians 6:11–12).

 Read Ephesians 6:11–12, and then describe an unseen spiritual battle for your soul.

When You Go Belly Up, You're in a Danger Zone!

Pay attention to what is happening around you, because your life is the enemy's playground. Here are some things that will help you.

- Be in tune with yourself spiritually instead of aimlessly going through the motions of life.
- Take care of your soul and spirit. Spend time in the Word and in prayer. Spend time with Christian friends who can encourage you, especially when you feel cast down.
- Realize the enemy likes to use people to get at you. He uses them to hurt you, discourage you, and yes, he sometimes uses other Christians to do that to you.
- Refuse to let Satan use you as a pawn in his game. Don't allow him to use you to mistreat someone who is mistreating you. That's the enemy, and you'll discourage another soul.
- Hold your tongue, even when someone upsets you. Satan loves it when you use words to hurt others.

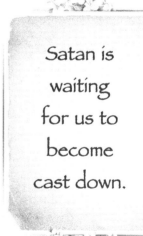

Satan is waiting for us to become cast down.

- Keep your eyes fastened on Jesus at all times. Satan will try to make you doubt or feel afraid. His agenda is to devour the Shepherd's daughter.

Any person who thinks he stands must be careful that he doesn't fall—even the Shepherd's daughter (cf. 1 Corinthians 10:12).

Life to My Soul

Be vigilant for your soul, which encompasses your mind and your heart, where your true self resides. You are not a body—you are a soul and a spirit. A poster states: "You don't have a soul, you are a soul. You have a body. The soul and the spirit are eternal."[8]

 What three parts of our created state does Paul mention in 1 Thessalonians 5:23–24?

 Why does Paul make a distinction there?

 How can one affect another?

The Hebrew word for soul is *nephesh*, meaning heart, life, and mind. God breathed life into Adam's nostrils and "man became a living soul" (Genesis 2:7 KJV). David uses the same word in Psalm 23:3.

If we take the literal translation of *restores*, meaning "He causes my life to return," and we add soul [*nephesh*], meaning the heart and mind, we can say it like this: "He causes life to return to my soul—my heart and my mind." Only the Good Shepherd can restore the soul. He is the one who can bring renewed vitality to our minds.

---

8 William O'Flaherty, "Top 10 Lines Falsely attributed to C. S. Lewis," *Christianity Today*, November 22, 1027. https://www.christianitytoday.com/ct/2017/november-web-only/top-10-misquoted-lines-from-cs-lewis.html.

How Does the Shepherd Restore the Sheep?

When a shepherd reaches a cast-down sheep, he immediately begins to massage the sheep's legs to restore blood circulation. He will talk calmly to the sheep in order to reassure him. Then the shepherd will gently lift the sheep upon his feet, sometimes straddling the sheep to ensure that he can stand on his own. Can you hear the shepherd saying, "When are you going to learn to stand on your own feet?" As a shepherd lovingly restores his sheep, so the Good Shepherd restores our souls.

> Only the Good Shepherd can restore the soul. He is the one who can bring renewed vitality.

David understood being cast down in his soul. He had been through so many ups and downs. I know he had days when he had more than he could take, and he made choices that he regretted. He had his share of laughter and summit experiences. He put down a Philistine giant and was praised by thousands for killing him. He fought and won many battles as king. He led Israel into a great season of blessings.

But we must be reminded that David had many sorrows, tears, and troubled times. He won; he lost; he got it right—sometimes. David experienced joy and regret, but he knew that God had been with him through all of it. That is the great message of the Twenty-third Psalm. David's words remind us that our Shepherd is always near, ready to set us on our feet again. And a good shepherd is always busy counting sheep to make sure none are missing.

From the Mouth of the Good Shepherd

What does the Good Shepherd do when a sheep is lost? He leaves ninety-nine and tenderly searches for one. That is how important one soul is to the Lord.

When we go missing—physically, spiritually, emotionally, mentally—the Good Shepherd is concerned for us.

> What man of you, having a hundred sheep, if he loses one of them, does not leave the ninety-nine in the wilderness, and go after the one which is lost until he finds it? And when he has found it, he lays it on his shoulders, rejoicing likewise there will be more joy in heaven over one sinner who repents than over ninety-nine just persons who need no repentance (Luke 15:4–7).

Dear reader, I have been belly up and cast down like that pitiful sheep more times than I can count. One thing I am sure of is that my Shepherd has always rescued me. It has happened time and time again. All I can do is praise Him for restoring me. Just as Aunt Alpha's old wardrobe was restored, He can bring us back from broken to beautiful. God can restore what is broken and change it into something amazing.

Sheep Homework

1. Recite the Twenty-third Psalm. Realize the benefits.

2. Meditate on Joel 2:25. Allow God to take the broken pieces of your life and change them into something amazing.

3. Who can you help that may be cast down? Send a card; make a phone call; pay a visit. Do something.

From Ruts to
Righteousness

Paths of Righteousness

Recite the Twenty-third Psalm.

At the end, add, "Oh, the benefits of being the Shepherd's daughter."

Sheep must be led to different pastures constantly, and there are good reasons. Like humans, sheep are creatures of habit. They are notorious for following the same trails until those trails become ruts. They will graze the same hills until the land is barren, and they will pollute their own ground until it is infested with disease and parasites. Sheep love to lie down in the same spots. That is why sheep need an excellent manager who protects them by moving them from pasture to pasture.

An intelligent shepherd is aware that the welfare of his sheep is at stake, not only for their health but also for the land. An excellent manager watches the balance between the growth and the grazing of his sheep. As soon as the maximum benefit is reached, he moves them off to a fresh field. Thus, "He leads me in the paths of righteousness," the paths of "right living."

The idea behind this verse, "He leads me in the paths of righteousness," is that the sheep are willing to be led out of a pitiful pasture into a better one. Isn't that the way of the Lord? Always wanting the very best for His children.

Who is the one who leads? Who should follow? We like doing things our own way. Following isn't our nature. We like our same old habits, and we get ruffled if we are interrupted. How do I know that? Well, just let someone take a member's seat as we assemble for worship and see what happens. Or let someone take a preferred parking place. Or change the order of any tradition.

The Comfort of Ruts

We get into ruts with our morning routine, our work routines, and our routines as a family. At our house, I cannot change one thing about our Christmas routine or the girls get upset.

Up at 4:00 AM, put on the coffee, put the sausage balls in the oven. Then Jenna begins dividing the presents. (She gets upset if anyone tries to take her job.) Everyone has a personal stack of gifts. No one can start opening gifts until everyone is there. We all have matching pajamas, except Arvy; he refuses. We open presents one at a time and go around the room. It takes a few hours. Then the breakfast casserole goes into the oven with more sausage balls. There are certain reindeer plates and mugs we must use.

There can be no changes, not even a hint of deviation or the girls start complaining. They like the same routine every year. Yes, we are in a "Christmas rut."

Do you see what I mean now about sheep? They like their routines just as we do.

 What are some of your "ruts"?

 Spiritually, how can ruts be harmful for us?

Spiritual Ruts

When I think of spiritual ruts, I think of the churches in the book of Revelation. Notice these churches and their spiritual ruts. Can we fall into the same ruts? Read about each of the seven churches in Revelation 2–3, and pay particular attention to their spiritual ruts. I have chosen two of the churches mentioned.

Ephesus

> Nevertheless I have this against you, that you have left your first love. Remember therefore from where you have fallen; repent and do the first works, or else I will come to you quickly and remove your lampstand from its place—unless you repent (Revelation 2:4–5).

 The church at Ephesus was in a spiritual rut. What was it?

 What is the cure?

 How do we, like the church at Ephesus, need to see our own ruts?

Laodicea

> I know your works, that you are neither cold nor hot. I could wish you were cold or hot. So then, because you are lukewarm, and neither cold nor hot, I will vomit you out of My mouth (Revelation 3:15–16).

 In what spiritual rut was the church at Laodicea?

 Were the members following a leader or going their own way?

 What had taken their focus away from God (Revelation 3:17)?

 What might cause us to need spiritual eye salve, especially when it comes to our own ruts and habits (Revelation 3:18)?

Can we have spiritual blind spots? If so, how can we recognize them?

Follow Instructions

Have you ever had to follow instructions as though your life depended on it? One man did.

> Robert Kupferschmid was an eighty-one-year-old with no flying experience. However, due to a tragic emergency, he was forced to fly an airplane. On June 17, 1998, he and his fifty-two-year-old pilot friend, Wesley Sickle, were flying from Indianapolis to Muncie, Indiana. During the flight, the pilot slumped over and died at the controls. The Cessna 172 single-engine plane began to nose-dive and Kupferschmid grabbed the controls. He got on the radio and pleaded for help.
>
> Nearby were two pilots who heard the call. Mount Comfort was the closest airport, and the two pilots gave Kupferschmid a steady stream of instructions of climbing, steering—and the scariest part—landing. The two experienced pilots had Kupferschmid circle the runway three times before this somewhat frantic and totally inexperienced pilot was ready to attempt the landing.
>
> Emergency vehicles were called out and ready for what seemed like an approaching disaster. Witnesses said the plane's nose nudged the center line and bounced a few times before the tail hit the ground. The Cessna ended up in a patch of soggy grass next to the runway. Amazingly, Kupferschmid was not injured.
>
> This pilot listened and followed those instructions as if his life depended on it—and it did.[9]

Can you imagine the instructor saying "turn right" and Kupferschmid saying, "Could I pray about it first?" Can you imagine the flight instructor saying "pull up" and hearing, "I don't feel like it." Or can you imagine Kupferschmid arguing or ignoring the least of the instructions of the pilots when his life was hanging in the balance?

---

9 "Sermon Illustration," SermonCentral.com, June 18, 2017. https://www.sermoncentral.com /sermon-illustrations/60235/robert-kupferschmid-was-an-81-year-old-with-no-by-sermoncentral.

He took every word seriously. He didn't debate; he didn't wait to put their instructions into action. He knew that following the instructions was his only hope of arriving alive.

Following Jesus down the paths of right living is our only hope for a good life here and peace in the hereafter.

Our Only Hope: Follow the Shepherd

We constantly see broken homes, broken marriages, broken hearts, and the effects of going our own way. The greed and jealousy of mankind cause us to live in a sin-sick society. I like things on a kindergarten level—easy to understand. Maybe the solution for our society is to go back to an old-fashioned game of "Follow the Leader." You know that game: The group selects a leader and all the players do what the leader tells them.

"Stomp your feet!" The players stomp their feet.

"Clap your hands!" The players clap their hands.

"Nod your head!" You guessed it; the players nod their heads.

We have a leader, and His name is Jesus. We are told over and over to follow Him, be like Him, think like Him, imitate Him. He gives us a simple lesson of "Follow the Leader" in the gospel of John:

> Most assuredly, I say to you, he who does not enter the sheepfold by the door, but climbs up some other way, the same is a thief and a robber. But he who enters by the door is the shepherd of the sheep. To him the doorkeeper opens, and the sheep hear his voice; and he calls his own sheep by name and leads them out. And when he brings out his own sheep, he goes before them; and the sheep follow him, for they know his voice. Yet they will by no means

Following Jesus down the paths of right living is our only hope for a good life here and peace in the hereafter.

follow a stranger, but will flee from him, for they do not know the voice of strangers (John 10:1–5).

My sheep hear My voice, and I know them, and they follow Me. And I give them eternal life, and they shall never perish; neither shall anyone snatch them out of My hand. My Father, who has given them to Me, is greater than all; and no one is able to snatch them out of My Father's hand. I and My Father are one (John 10:27–30).

 Whose voice do the sheep recognize?

 Who are they following? Is he the leader?

 What does the Shepherd give the sheep?

It's really simple when it comes to being led in a path of right living. The Lord our Shepherd will never lead us on the wrong path. He has only the best in mind for us and He wants to see us flourish as His sheep.

How do we know His path? He has given it to us in His Word. We can't follow His path if we don't know His path. When we are on the path of righteousness, we understand that our sin breaks God's heart. We become concerned about the sins we commit. Our hearts should be broken when we sin because we realize our sins bring shame to our Good Shepherd's name.

Whoever commits sin also commits lawlessness, and sin is lawlessness (1 John 3:4).

 What is sin?

 How can we be in a certain rut with our sin?

 Do you have a certain habitual sin? What steps can you take to get rid of it?

Walk in These Spiritual Ruts

But if we walk in the light as He is in the light, we have fellowship with one another, and the blood of Jesus Christ His Son cleanses us from all sin (1 John 1:7).

He who says he abides in Him ought himself also to walk just as He walked (1 John 2:6).

Do not love the world or the things in the world. If anyone loves the world, the love of the Father is not in him (1 John 2:15).

Why is the world's path not safe to follow?

How should we walk, as His sheep?

What happens when we do the Father's will?

Must we follow His will to be in the path of righteousness? Why or why not?

John was the apostle of love. He did not write out of anger or resentment, but out of a loving heart, as a warning so that we will take note of our walk. We have to put on our spiritual walking shoes and learn to follow the Shepherd down the path of right living. When it comes to our relationship with God, there is no room for error. It's like a pilot's coming in for a landing. If he doesn't do it right the first time, there wouldn't be a second time. He must get it right. So must we!

Why is that so important for today? Because we live in a time when many religions have embraced a kind of gospel that makes it possible for people to profess Christ and be in the world at the same time without any conviction of conscience.

> He has only the best in mind for us and He wants to see us flourish as His sheep.

In theology there is a term called *easy believe-ism.* It means "show up for worship, say a word, say a prayer, and then go on doing what you want to do." In easy believe-ism, there is not a desire to be led by the Shepherd, and certainly not a willingness to follow Him. There is not a desire for the easy-believe-ism Christian to repent and admit, "I have sinned against God and the church." The desire is, "I'll do whatever I want to do." We might be fooling ourselves, but we are not fooling God.

 Where does *easy believe-ism* lead?

 Discuss how *easy believe-ism* can be a rut.

Spiritually, what happens when we move from our ruts to the right paths with the Good Shepherd?

- We experience renewed hope. No ruts of distrust!
- We have a better outlook on our future. No ruts of negativity!
- We are ready to serve Him. No more ruts of saying, "Let someone else do it!"
- We lay aside sins that cause us to stumble. No ruts of sinful behavior!
- We are willing to learn and grow as we walk with God. No ruts of neglecting Bible study and quiet time with God!
- We follow Him to new experiences and new opportunities! No ruts of "I'm too afraid to try!"

Nothing pleases our Good Shepherd more than to see His sheep follow Him from ruts to righteousness.

Lord, lead me on from day to day; I will follow You all the way!

Sheep Homework

1. Recite the Twenty-third Psalm and remember the benefits.

2. Meditate on John 10:27. Write it down. Memorize it.

3. Identify your ruts and do something about them. Start today.

4. What would you tell someone who asks, "What are the benefits of following the Good Shepherd?"

5. Ponder being held in His perfect will as you follow Him down the right paths. How does this bring you comfort?

Ten Signs Your Christianity
Has Become Too Comfortable

1. You attend church but with little expectancy.

2. You no longer seem concerned about the spiritual condition of your family members, neighbors, and co-workers.

3. You haven't had a spiritual conversation with a non-Christian in a long time.

4. The Bible seems to be a lifeless book.

5. Your happiness on Sunday mornings is more important than what it takes to reach the lost. So long as you get your parking spot and your seat, and you hear the songs you like, everything is fine.

6. The plight of the poor doesn't concern you.

7. Pictures of those who are suffering do not move you to action.

8. You do not give sacrificially. When was the last time you increased your contribution?

9. Your prayer life is dead.

10. You never expect God to do something incredible in your life. It's not even on your radar.[10]

As the Shepherd's daughters, we must never get into a spiritual rut. We must follow Him from ruts to right living. After all, as Christians we do wear His name.

---

10 https://churchleaders.com/outreach-missions/outreach-missions-articles/161369-brian_dodd_10_signs_your_christianity_has_become_too_comfortable_outreach.html.

The Shepherd's

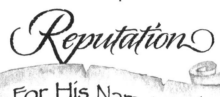

Reputation

For His Name's Sake

 Recite the Twenty-third Psalm.

At the end, add, "Oh, the benefits of being the Shepherd's daughter."

When David writes "He leads me in the paths of righteousness for His name's sake," he gives us a picture of the Shepherd's reputation. As the shepherd king, David understood that the owner's reputation was held in high esteem, if he was a good manager.

- Are his sheep healthy?
- Are they flourishing?
- Are they well-adjusted?
- Are they fearful or serene?
- Does he make sure the pastures are not over-grazed?

- Are the sheep free of friction and agitation within the flock?

How well the sheep flourish is completely dependent upon the shepherd, and the sheep's well-being reflects his care and provision.

His Name, His Honor

Let's go a little deeper here. Think spiritually with me. When we become His sheep, we put Him on like a garment (Galatians 3:27). We belong to Christ, and we wear His name, "Christian."

When we allow Him to lead us in the paths of right living, His fruit should be visible in our lives (Galatians 5:22–25). What do other people—sheep in other pastures that are not under the Good Shepherd's care—see in us? How well do we honor His name? Are we upholding our Shepherd's reputation?

> Therefore, if anyone is in Christ, he is a new creation; old things have passed away; behold, all things have become new . . . Now then, we are ambassadors for Christ, as though God were pleading through us: we implore you on Christ's behalf, be reconciled to God (2 Corinthians 5:17, 20).

What does Paul mean when he tells us, as God's new creation, that old things have passed away?

What is an ambassador?

How does He plead through us?

2 Corinthians 5:20 states: "Therefore, we are ambassadors for Christ, God making his appeal through us. We implore you on behalf of Christ, be reconciled to God" (ESV). What great responsibility does this place on us?

What responsibilities do we bear in our daily lives through our examples as Christ's sheep?

How do we show the world that we as His sheep are joyful, well-nourished, and confident?

Why should we exhibit the fruit of the Spirit in our lives (Galatians 5:22–24)?

What Am I Leaving Behind for His Name's Sake?

As we have seen, sheep require meticulous care and attention, and even the best sheep have bad traits. But did you know that sheep can be the most beneficial of all livestock, if properly managed?

In a few years, a flock of well-managed sheep will clean up and restore a piece of ravaged land as no other creature can do.[11] It has been said in ancient literature that sheep are referred to as "those with the golden hooves." I'm sure you're thinking, "Finally, something positive about these notoriously stubborn little creatures." I must say, knowing this makes me feel much better as one of His sheep. Just to think that the sheep make a unique and worthwhile contribution is heartwarming. They leave behind something productive, beautiful, and beneficial.

Philip Keller tell us:

> Their manure is the best balanced of any produced by domestic stock. When scattered efficiently over the pastures, it proves of enormous benefit to the soil. The sheep's habit of seeking highest rise of ground on which to

In a few years, a flock of well-managed sheep will clean up and restore a piece of ravaged land as no other creature can do.

---

11 Keller, *A Shepherd Looks at Psalm 23*, 131.

rest ensures that the fertility from the lowland is re-deposited on the less productive higher ground.[12]

Keller also writes that no other livestock consumes such a wide variety of herbage. Sheep eat all sorts of undesirable plants that might otherwise invade a field. For example, they love the buds and tender tips of Canada thistle which, if not controlled, can quickly become a most noxious weed.

William Shakespeare wrote, "The evil that men do lives after them; the good is oft interred with their bones."[13] Although there is kernel of truth in what Shakespeare said, the voice John heard from heaven said, "Blessed are the dead who die in the Lord . . . that they may rest from their labors, and their works follow them" (Revelation 14:13). What about us? For His name's sake shouldn't we, as His sheep, leave something good behind us?

> "How beautiful upon the mountains are the feet of him who brings good news, who proclaims peace" (Isaiah 52:7).

> "Blessed are the peacemakers, for they shall be called sons of God" (Matthew 5:9).

 Do I leave behind love or hatred?

 Do I leave behind forgiveness or a mean spirit?

 Do I leave behind contentment or confusion?

 Do I leave behind joy or frustration?

A Sweet Remembrance

Fragrances linger. One morning I was in our church supply room making copies for my class, and as usual, I was wearing my favorite perfume. One of

---

12 Ibid.

13 William Shakespeare, *Julius Caesar*, Act 3, scene ii.

the ladies approached me later and said, "I know you have been in the supply room because your frangrance lingers there." I smiled and asked, "Did you like the fragrance?" And she replied, "Yes, it is the sweeetest smelling perfume, and I want some too." The aroma of our lives for His name's sake, should lead others to Christ, because we are "sheep with golden hooves."

Sheep are expected to produce a profit for the shepherd.

Think about the relationship of sheep and shepherds for a moment. Is it not true that sheep exist for the benefit of the shepherd? Sheep are led into zones of comfort in order to be prepared for zones of discomfort. In other words, sheep are expected to produce a profit for the shepherd.

> Likewise, we, God's sheep, exist for God, the Shepherd. To change or alter that relationship in any way would turn us into idolaters, where we use God for our benefit, rather than allowing God to use us for his benefit. We live for him.[14]

There are benefits to being the Shepherd's daughter and living "for His name's sake," and we must show the world. Consider the Shepherd's reputation as you read the following qualities we must cultivate.

- Contentment is a mark of the Shepherd's daughter.

- Nourishment in the Word of God is a mark of the Shepherd's daughter.

- A joyful spirit and a pleasant countenance are marks of the Shepherd's daughter.

- A forgiving spirit is a mark of the Shepherd's daughter.

- Confidence and trust are marks of the Shepherd's daughter.

---

14 Rick Ezell, "Sermon: For His Name's Sake—Psalm 23," 01/01/14, https://www.lifeway.com/en /articles/sermon-power-praying-4-for-his-names-sake.

- Submission to the Shepherd is a mark of the Shepherd's daughter.

Everything we do and every word we speak reflects upon our Good Shepherd, and the world is watching. We are to live "for His name's sake."

Our Good Shepherd can walk on water and turn water into wine. He is the King of kings and the Lord of lords. He is the Prince of Peace, the Bread, the Door, and the Living Water. We belong to Him.

- He is the one who died on the cross for us!
- He is the one who rules our lives!
- He is the one who rules the universe!

When you wear the name *Christian*, you wear His name. You live for His name's sake, so proudly tell the world, "I am the Shepherd's daughter." And don't forget to tell the benefits of being His.

One particular morning, I was making Dad's breakfast when he asked me, "Why have you been so good to me?"

I said, "Dad, I'm not good on my own, but I can be good to you because I follow Jesus. He tells me to be good to others. I'm trying to follow what Jesus told me to do." Tears filled Dad's eyes.

Sometimes we make following Jesus difficult. When we surrender to His will and follow His ways, it becomes the easiest action we can do. Following Jesus is never about us. It's always about Him. There is nothing more secure for a child of God than being held in the arms of the Good Shepherd and complying to His will. The old familiar hymn, "I Have Decided to Follow Jesus," begins each of its four stanzas as follows.

1. I have decided to follow Jesus

2. The world behind me

3. Though none go with me, I still will follow

4. My cross I'll carry, till I see Jesus

But what makes that hymn so compelling is that at the end of each stanza is the phrase: "No turning back, no turning back."

We can follow Him out of the ruts of our lives down the perfect path of righteousness, because we bear His name to the world.

Oh, the benefits of being the Shepherd's daughter.

Sheep Homework

1. Considering that your conduct is "for His name's sake," how are you representing His name to the world? Make sure your walk matches your talk and vice versa.

2. Pray and ask God to help in your understanding of "His name's sake" and how it regulates your conduct as His sheep in the world.

3. Read Ephesians 2:10. What does this verse tell us about our "walk"?

4. Read Colossians 2:6–8. How can the things of this world keep us from living "for His name's sake"?

Sheep to Shepherd

Sheep Trials and Shepherd Provisions

SHEEP TO SHEPHERD
Sheep Trials and Shepherd Provisions

The Shepherd
of the Hills and Valleys

The Valley of the Shadow of Death

Recite the Twenty-third Psalm.

At the end, add, "Oh, the benefits of being the Shepherd's daughter."

It is the most reassuring and reinforcing experience to the child of God to discover that there is, even in the dark valley, a source of strength and courage to be found in God. It is when we look back over life and see how the Shepherd's hand has guided and sustained him in the darkest hours that renewed faith is engendered.[15]

When you walk through the hills and valleys of life, you must remember you are not alone. Sometimes you need the help of a professional, especially when trouble comes.

---

15 Keller, *A Shepherd Looks at Psalm 23*, 89.

A young mother hired a babysitter so she could run some errands. While shopping, the babysitter called: "Can you come home? And please hurry. Your baby is running a high fever!"

The mother was frantic. She rushed into a pharmacy to pick up some needed medication. And would you believe she locked her keys in the car!

She panicked and ran to a phone. The babysitter said, "Oh my, the baby's fever has gotten worse. You've got to come home now."

Then the babysitter hesitated and calmly suggested, "Why don't you go inside and ask for a coat hanger? I'm sure they have people locking their keys inside their cars all the time."

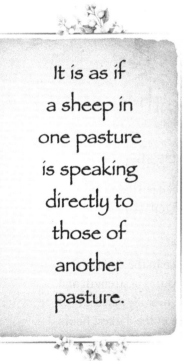

It is as if a sheep in one pasture is speaking directly to those of another pasture.

The mother quickly found a coat hanger and returned to her car and in frustration: "I don't know how to use this. I've never tried to get keys out of a car before." She bowed her head, and she asked God to send help. Soon a dirty, greasy, bearded motorcyclist with an old biker skull rag on his head pulled up beside her.

The woman looked toward heaven and mumbled under her breath, "This is who you send to help me?" But she was desperate so she was thankful.

"Can I help you?" he asked as he dismounted.

"Yes, my daughter is very sick at home and I stopped to get medicine. I've locked my keys inside the car. Do you know how to use this coat hanger?"

In less than a minute the stranger opened her door. She hugged him and through tears she said, "Thank you! Thank you! I appreciate you so much; you are such a nice man!"

The man replied, "Lady, I'm not a nice man. About an hour ago I was released from prison for car theft."

Then the grateful mother hugged the man again and cried out, "Oh thank You, God! You even sent me a professional!"

Our Shepherd is a professional, and He knows exactly what He is doing.

Remember, the sheep and the shepherd have a close relationship, even to the point that the shepherd will give his life for the sheep if necessary. That's what a good shepherd does. He's a professional.

Yea though I walk through the valley of the shadow of death, I will fear no evil; for You are with me; Your rod and Your staff, they comfort me.

—Psalm 23:4

It's Mine! Pronouns Worth Noting

Notice the pronouns, *I, me, my,* in Psalm 23:1–3. It is as if a sheep in one pasture is speaking directly to those of another pasture. Verses 1–3 represent springtime with the sheep. The green pastures and still waters represent the beginning of a relationship with the shepherd.

Now look at the pronouns, *you* and *your,* in verses 4–6. They've changed. The sheep now addresses the shepherd directly. Verses 4–6 represent different seasons with the shepherd: summer, fall, and winter.

Verse 4 begins the summer season. It is common practice for shepherds to divide the year and take their flocks to distant summer ranges in the high country for grazing, until late fall. Finding good pasture and water and then safely moving his sheep isn't easy.

As the flock moves to new feeding ground, the relationship between the sheep and the shepherd becomes more personal and intimate. Why? Because the journey often takes them through difficult valleys. The sheep and the shepherd will spend months together in close companionship. The sheep will be in the solitary care of the shepherd.

No more lying around in green pastures, no more resting beside still waters. The time has come when each sheep must depend on the shepherd for its life.

How does the "springtime" of green pastures and still waters represent our lives when things seem to be going well?

How can we sometimes experience aggravation, hard treks or rough terrain, in the green pastures of home?

Think back to a time in your life when things were "smooth sailing" on a still sea. How close to the Shepherd were you during this time?

The Valley Experience

The shepherd leaves the pastures of home and leads his flock through the mountain range. The sheep will feed as they gradually work their way up the mountainside. The higher the climb, the more dangerous the journey.

Picture the shepherd coming for the sheep and saying, "It's time to move, my little flock. You have to stay close beside me; you have to listen to me; there can't be any foolishness now; you've got to depend on me for your life."

This is a time when danger is ever present. The shepherd moves the sheep over cliffs and rough rocks. The terrain is difficult. Wolves and mountain lions threaten the flock, thus the "shadow" of death is all around them. This is not a time for foolishness in the flock. The sheep must stay close to the shepherd, or they will get hurt or even killed. This verse isn't speaking of death but the presence of it—the shadow of death.

Are shadows real? Well, yes and no. A shadow is the image of something being cast onto something else. Something is causing the shadow. The shadow represents the presence of evil. In this case the shadow of death is the presence of mountain lions, coyotes, and wolves. As long as the sheep walk with the shepherd, nothing bad is going to happen to them.

Let's turn our minds back to the characteristics of sheep. Do the sheep have any weapons or means of defense? No! They are completely dependent upon the shepherd. Remember, they have no sharp teeth, no claws. And their legs are too short to outrun any predator. Can you imagine these little sheep climbing a mountainside?

The sheep have come to realize that the shepherd goes before them. He leads them. They know they have to follow him and stay close to him. They participate in a daily walk with the shepherd.

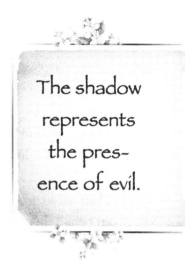

The shadow represents the presence of evil.

Ponder the thought that you are a defenseless sheep. In what ways do you depend upon the Shepherd?

Why must you stay close to the Shepherd?

What is different in this summer season compared to the "green pastures and still waters" season?

How can you relate this to your own life?

The Shepherd's Weapon and Guide

The last part of verse 4 says, "Your rod and Your staff, they comfort me." The rod is a weapon of defense, similar to a club, to defend the sheep against hungry predators. The sheep feel comforted because they know the shepherd will protect them. The staff was used as a guide to direct the sheep. It was also used to rescue the sheep and pull them back when they got into trouble. The staff was also a separating tool.

When we get into trouble spiritually, what is our weapon (Hebrews 4:12)?

What assurance does Romans 8:11 promise?

What promise did our Shepherd make to His apostles regarding His guidance after His departure (John 16:13)?

When we do not know how to pray properly, what does the Spirit do on our behalf (Romans 8:26–27)?

As Jesus' sheep, we will walk through difficult places too. We will climb the mountains of adversity and go through valleys of despair and disappointment, and we will come near the cliffs and rough edges of life.

We are always, as long as we live, going to face obstacles, but David reminds us: "Yea, though I walk through the valley . . . You are with me."

Three Important Words

David uses three words to help us understand the "valley experience": *though, walk,* and *through.* You need to value the importance of these three words when you face the "valley."

The word *though* means to expect, that is, not be surprised or shocked when a valley experience happens. We live on a fallen green and blue planet. Read Romans 8:18–21 to help you understand why this third rock from the sun is a fallen place.

We live subject to the things of this world: poor health, unfortunate accidents, and bad circumstances. Most of these things are out of our control. I do not mean for this to sound like doomsday has arrived, but I do want us to understand that life happens. That doesn't mean we have to go around thinking the worst, but it does mean that we will face trials, obstacles, and unforeseen events.

- Our bodies were not made to last forever.

- Our bodies are subject to all the conditions of the earth.

- Our bodies have nerves and brain cells, so we are affected by problems, heartaches, and disappointments.

- We shouldn't be surprised when a valley experience occurs.

The Bible helps us understand that on this earth bad things can happen to good people.

- Job 14:1: "Man who is born of woman is of few days and full of trouble."

- James 1:2: "Count it all joy when you fall into various trials."

- 1 Peter 1:6: "In this you greatly rejoice, though now for a little while, if need be, you have been grieved by various trials."

- Romans 12:12: "Rejoice in hope, be patient in tribulation, be constant in prayer" (ESV).

 What do these verses teach us about the discouraging circumstances of our lives?

Valley Experiences

The one who falls and gets up is much stronger
than the one who never fell.[16]

As already stated, Psalm 23 became my go-to and my strength during my dad's long illness and stroke. During his time of suffering I faced so many obstacles, so many trials, and so many setbacks. My life was like Clint Eastwood's movie: *The Good, the Bad, and the Ugly!*

My dad's negative reaction to the doctors who cared for him brought added stress to my life. I often felt as if I were in a deep dark valley. As every daughter who loves her daddy no matter what, I just wanted him to

---

16 Author unknown, motivatequotes.com.

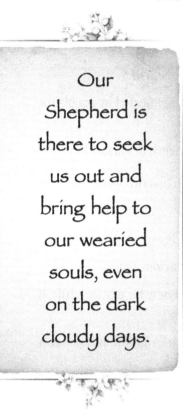

Our Shepherd is there to seek us out and bring help to our wearied souls, even on the dark cloudy days.

get better. I wanted to help him, but he refused to cooperate. He felt as if he were thirty in an eighty-two-year-old body!

Within three months of Dad's stroke, my brother-in-law, Cegal, had a terrible accident. Two days prior to the accident, he and my sister and their two children, ages eight and five, had moved into a beautiful new home.

They moved in before the railing had been installed upstairs on the ten-foot balcony. That particular night, they had been cleaning and working on the house, and decided to move the large saws in the den below outside. They had worked long and hard that day. Around midnight my sister went to bed with the two children. My brother-in-law worked a little longer, and then went to bed upstairs.

We still don't know exactly what happened, because my brother-in-law cannot remember. We think he was sleepwalking or otherwise disoriented, but somehow, only a few hours later, he stepped off that ten-foot balcony and fell to the hardwood floors below. Thank the Lord, the saws had been removed!

At 2:00 AM our phone rang. It was Mother. She told us that Cegal was being transported by plane to the university hospital, UAB in Birmingham. Through her tears she said, "He is serious and he may not make it." Our hearts were broken. I will never forget that night as long as I live.

The short version of that tragedy is that my brother-in-law suffered a spinal cord injury that left him paralyzed from the waist down. Life changed for our family that day, and especially for my sister, her husband Cegal, and their children. It seemed as though we had more than our share of burdens, problems, and unfortunate events at that time. It was devastating for me to visit my dad and tell him this terrible news. He just kept saying through tears, "I'm so sorry, I'm so sorry."

Our family was experiencing "even though."

As cliché as Forrest Gump's famous line has become, it is absolutely true. Like a box of chocolates, none of us know from one minute to the next what we will get. But one thing we can know is that *though* means to expect life to change.

> My Sorrow, when she's here with me,
> Thinks these dark days of autumn rain
> Are beautiful as days can be;
> She loves the bare, the withered tree;
> She walks the sodden pasture lane.
>
> —Robert Frost[17]

How can we cope more patiently with trials by knowing that life can change?

Should we expect our lives always to be easy or problem free? Why or why not?

How is it a dishonor to our Shepherd to adopt the attitude that life is nothing but a "series of unfortunate events"?

The Shepherd Is Always with Us

As the Shepherd's daughters, our attitudes should always be those of gratitude and thankfulness to God for all He provides. He is there to seek us out and bring help to our wearied souls, even on the dark cloudy days.

> As a shepherd seeks out his flock on the day he is among his scattered sheep, so will I seek out My sheep and deliver them from all the places where they were scattered on a cloudy and dark day (Ezekiel 34:12).

---

17 Robert Frost, "My November Guest," *A Boy's Will*, 1913. https://beamingnotes.com/2013/05/21 /my-november-guest-analysis-by-robert-frost/.

How does Ezekiel 34:12 bring comfort to your heart?

 What kind of day is mentioned in this passage?

 What life-lessons have you learned from "cloudy and dark" days?

One of the most beautiful sequences in this psalm are the words, "You are with me." In addition to Psalm 23:4, the following scriptures also instruct us that He is always with us, no matter what.

> For He Himself has said, "I will never leave you nor forsake you." So we may boldly say: "The Lord is my helper; I will not fear. What can man do to me?" (Hebrews 13:5–6).

 How does knowing you are not alone in the "valley experiences" of life help you?

Walk! Don't Camp in the Valley

The second word we must contemplate is *walk*. Walk is an important word because it does not indicate we quit or stop, but rather that we keep moving. We take one step at a time and focus on our Shepherd. The idea is that we pace ourselves. When a tragedy happens or we experience a sudden loss of someone we love, or whatever the "valley" is, it takes time to process the pain. Grief, hurt, and heartbreak are different for everyone.

I'll never forget the harsh words spoken to a friend after losing her mother. A coworker said, "You need to get over it, move on, and stop being so depressed." That wasn't easy because she and her mom were very close. My friend felt the pain of her mom's absence, and her heart was broken. The coworker needed to be more sensitive to her valley experience. Although we do need to keep moving, we all move at our own pace.

Walk means we don't stay in the valley. I don't know about you, but my inclinations are just to stop. Retreat. Pull back. Go into my cocoon, as a caterpillar spins itself into webs of protection and isolation. David made it clear when he wrote "I walk through," because he understood the valley experience. He meant we don't pitch a tent, camp out, or stay there. We have to keep walking and keep moving, but it is a process.

 Identify your methods of dealing with the "valley experience." How is it *through* vs. *withdrawn?*

The Lord Ain't Finished Yet!

I know that *ain't* isn't proper grammar, but it is a word, so I'll use it. When we are in a valley, we have to say this and remember it: "The Lord ain't finished with me yet!" He is doing His work. He is helping us as we "walk" through the valley.

My brother-in-law amazes me. In spite of being paralyzed, he has not let his accident stop him from enjoying life and moving on. He would be the first to tell you that it's not the life he envisioned, but he didn't let it stop him. He works every day. He is a chiropractor, and he adjusts from his wheelchair. He has kept moving. He could have sat in his house every day and been depressed over his circumstances. Instead he chose to keep moving forward.

Cegal loves people and cares about their souls. He is always encouraging others and helping them with their problems. If they can't afford chiropractic care, he helps them with that too. His whole perspective in life changed after the accident. He now realizes that God has a purpose for him as he "walks" every day with the Lord's help.

There is a season for hurt and pain in the valley, but we move on because we know the Shepherd isn't finished yet. He is doing His work. We have to

> David made it clear when he wrote "I walk through." He understood the valley experience.

hold on and trust Him. His hands are capable and His comfort is real. Just say in your valley, "The Lord ain't finished with me yet!"

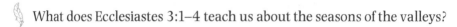 What does Ecclesiastes 3:1–4 teach us about the seasons of the valleys?

Why are we to keep moving (Philippians 3:14)?

How should we respond when someone is processing pain (Romans 12:15)?

Focus on the Shepherd and Encourage Yourself

In the valley experience, our focus often gets off balance. We need to be keenly aware of how we are feeling: When we are heartbroken, tired, and overwhelmed, it is during these times we must remember that valley experiences leave us vulnerable, spiritually.

- Are we overly anxious?
- Are we short-tempered and angry?
- Do we take our hurt and frustration out on other people?
- Are we withdrawing and unsocial?
- Have we lost our joy?

When we find ourselves in these seasons beyond our control, it is most important for us to focus our attention on the Good Shepherd. A valley experience is a good time for us to counsel ourselves with the word of truth. If our goal is to walk with our Shepherd and go to heaven, then we need to "encourage ourselves."

I happen to think self-counsel and self-encouragement are healthy spiritual practices. After all, that is exactly what David did.

Now David was greatly distressed, for the people spoke of stoning him, because the soul of all the people was grieved, every man for his sons and his daughters. But David strengthened himself in the Lord his God (1 Samuel 30:6).

Some translations use *encouraged* instead of *strengthened.*

Sometimes people don't notice when we are in a valley. They are working through too many problems of their own. And even if they do notice, some don't know what to say.

When I become depressed and want to quit walking, I say to myself, "Debbie, you know better than this. You know who your God is. You know what He can do. You know how He wants you to respond. You know He has work for you to do." Then I encourage myself from the word of God. I read and repeat the promises of God because they are true.

 How can we encourage ourselves in the Lord?

 How can we tell ourselves the truth about who we are in the Lord?

 Why is this a wise practice?

Staying in My Lane

I once thought, "I must always accept my circumstances," but that is not true. If we are in a valley experience with people who are draining us mentally by hurting us or being unreasonable, we must think of ourselves. Sometimes that means establishing a boundary. Or it might mean that we wish them well, pray for them, and remain kind, but we must take care of ourselves spiritually. Jesus established a boundary when He sent the Twelve to the lost sheep of the house of Israel. "And if anyone will not receive you or listen to your words, shake off the dust from your feet when you leave that house or town" (Matthew 10:14 ESV). Whatever it takes to reach our goal of heaven, we must do.

It's hard not to care about what other people think or do, but more important, I want to please the Lord. He is my goal. Heaven is my goal, so whatever I need to do spiritually to keep walking, that is what I do. I call it "staying in my own lane."

The following verse encourages us to keep watching, hoping, and waiting for the first light of dawn. That means we just keep "walking through."

> The path of the righteous is like the light of dawn, which shines brighter and brighter until full day (Proverbs 4:18 ESV).

Cross Over

We must remember as we walk that life keeps changing. Better days are ahead. Hold on to that thought.

The valley is a season. Seasons change. Seasons end. Right? We keep that as our focus and don't allow our circumstances to make us bitter. Don't let yesterday use up too much of today. Sometimes God closes doors because it's time to move forward. He knows you won't move unless your circumstances force you. You can't start the next chapter of your life if you keep rereading the last one.

The Lord often says, "Get moving!" When God's people of old experienced valleys, He commanded, "Cross over."

> "Now rise and cross over the Valley of the Zered." So we crossed over the Valley of the Zered (Deuteronomy 2:13).

 Research Deuteronomy 2:13, 24; 11:11; and Jeremiah 15:14. How did "crossing over" produce a change of circumstance?

Through the Valley

The word *through* indicates there is an end in sight. We must keep the end in view and realize the path to higher ground is not a dead-end street. What is the end for the Christian? Heaven.

Have you ever had a day when you couldn't see an end in sight? Often the difficulties and urgent crises of life can make the days stretch endlessly. But we cannot be God's complete work without trials (James 1:2–4). God always has a purpose in mind.

As C. S. Lewis states, "If you think of this world as a place intended simply for our happiness, you find it quite intolerable; think of it as a place of training and correction and it's not so bad." [18]

The Good Shepherd always has in mind the best interests of His sheep. He knows He can't leave them in one place if they are going to find their purpose. He moves them through rough terrain to get them to better places.

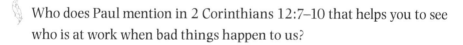

> And lest I should be exalted above measure by the abundance of the revelations, a thorn in the flesh was given to me, a messenger of Satan to buffet me, lest I be exalted above measure. Concerning this thing I pleaded with the Lord three times that it might depart from me. And He said to me, "My grace is sufficient for you, for My strength is made perfect in weakness." Therefore most gladly I will rather boast in my infirmities, that the power of Christ may rest upon me. Therefore I take pleasure in infirmities, in reproaches, in needs, in persecutions, in distresses, for Christ's sake. For when I am weak, then I am strong (2 Corinthians 12:7–10).

Who does Paul mention in 2 Corinthians 12:7–10 that helps you to see who is at work when bad things happen to us?

When is our strength made perfect?

What happens when we begin to look at our trials and obstacles as training grounds?

You can't start the next chapter of your life if you keep rereading the last one.

---

18 C. S. Lewis, *God in the Dock* (Grand Rapids, MI: Eerdmans Publishing Co., 2014), 41.

What does Romans 8:28 teach us? What does "all" mean?

Look to the Shepherd

We should always look to our Shepherd to guide and protect us, because it is our nature as sheep to try to handle our own problems. The Good Shepherd says, "Now wait a minute, my little sheep. You have to depend on Me if you are going to get from this valley to the mountaintop." Can you hear Him say, "Stay close; don't leave Me and I will never leave you"? He wants us to trust His leading, His protection, and His plan.

When we go through the valley, we can't see all that God is doing, and sometimes life's disruptions and troubles don't make sense. When my dad was ill those three-and-a-half years, I felt so completely fearful and completely ambushed. I thought, "How can anything good come out of this?" But I came to realize, as the Shepherd's daughter, that in every trial, every problem, every disease, every accident, every disappointment, every dark, cloudy, and difficult day, and every circumstance beyond my control, God was doing His work and weaving a beautiful picture of my life.

We look at life from the underside of a beautiful tapestry. The view gives us a jumbled confusing picture, and we can't seem to make sense of it. When our life becomes like the underside of the tapestry, we begin to question God: "How, God? Why, God? What are You doing, God? Where are You, God, in all of this confusion?"

But when we turn the beautiful tapestry over, we see the big extraordinarily woven tapestry—a breathtaking view. We then visualize how those tiny strings are woven, strings that didn't make sense before, and we are astounded.

Can you hear the Good Shepherd say, "Now, My little sheep, I know exactly what I am doing. All you have to do is trust Me."

"The Weaver," also known as "The Tapestry Poem," was often quoted by Corrie Ten Boom, who experienced many valley days during the darkness of

the Holocaust. She and her sister, Betsie, were taken to a concen
because they helped Jews escape the Nazi's during World War I

The Weaver

My life is but a weaving
Between my God and me.
I cannot choose the colors
He weaveth steadily.

Oft times He weaveth sorrow;
And I in foolish pride
Forget He sees the upper
And I the underside.

Not 'til the loom is silent
And the shuttles cease to fly
Will God unroll the canvas
And reveal the reason why.

The dark threads are as needful
In the weaver's skillful hand
As the threads of gold and silver
In the pattern He has planned.

He knows, He loves, He cares;
Nothing this truth can dim.
He gives the very best to those
Who leave the choice to Him.

—Grant Colfax Tullar[19]

---

19 D. J. Edwardson, "The Tapestry Poem," Jan. 6, 2015. Accessed March 22, 2020. http://www
.djedwardson.com/tapestry-poem/.

Indeed, God is the God of the hills and valleys, and we are not alone. During my family's valley experience, my guide, helper, and protector was the Shepherd of the hills and the valleys.

Oh, the benefits of being the Shepherd's daughter.

Sheep Homework

1. Recite the Twenty-third Psalm.

2. Recount all the benefits of being the Shepherd's daughter at this point of the study.

3. Memorize and meditate upon Ezekiel 34:12 and record it here.

4. Remember three important words in the valley experience: *though, walk,* and *through.* Encourage someone this week, using these three words.

5. How do you plan to respond when a valley experience occurs in your life?

10

Come To the Table

In the Presence of My Enemies

 Recite the Twenty-third Psalm.
At the end, add, "Oh, the benefits
of being the Shepherd's daughter."

No matter the occasion, my grandmother was always preparing a table. She never dreamed of having a job outside the home. Her role was to make sure that the needs of everyone in the family were met. I cannot count the times I helped her get the table ready for a meal.

When Grandmother told me, "Debbie, set the table." I interpreted, "Get the table ready for a feast." I anticipated the coming spread: Fried potato squares with gravy and onions, a large pot of pinto beans cooked slowly to perfection, cornbread that melted in your mouth, and sweet tea made like no one else's. And don't forget the lemon slices.

At her command, I would grab the plates, glasses, silverware, and napkins. She prepared the meal, but I prepared the table.

Keep the following questions in mind as we prepare to draw parallels between Grandmother's table and our Shepherd's tableland.

What is the difference in preparing the meal and setting the table?

How do we share our lives with one another as we share the meal?

What kind of preparation is needed when you host a meal for an invited guest?

Name at least three occasions when you "set the table."

To live is to live richly.
To walk here is to walk with quiet assurance.
To feed here is to be replete with good things.
To find this tableland is to find something of my Shepherd's love for me.[20]

The Tableland

As we turn our thoughts to the statement, "You prepare a table before me in the presence of my enemies," let's think of the shepherd and the sheep. A good shepherd is always making preparations. He goes ahead of the sheep to prepare the "table" or grazing area.

At this point of the psalm, the sheep are approaching the high mountain country of the summer ranges. David draws attention to the new grazing land of an area that is a flat pasture on a mountain. It may be that he is

---

20 Keller, *A Shepherd Looks at Psalm 23*, 113.

referring to a high, hard-to-reach plateau or mesa. The shepherd goes ahead early in the season to prepare the tableland for the sheep.

Preparing the table is no accident. The shepherd has planned it in advance. The job is meticulous, tedious, and tiring. He takes salt and other minerals for distribution and locates the best grazing spots. He frees the chosen area from weeds with the nutrition of the sheep in mind. He scouts the range and surveys the landscape to make sure he can protect his sheep from predators.

 Concerning sheep, what is the "table"?

 What preparations are involved as the shepherd goes ahead to prepare the table?

The Enemies of the Summer Range

As the shepherd carefully plans the beautiful pasture, he will be on the lookout for substances that are dangerous to the sheep.

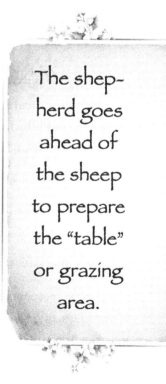

The shepherd goes ahead of the sheep to prepare the "table" or grazing area.

- *Poisonous plants*—Certain weeds are poisonous and can be fatal for the sheep if they are ingested. Some of those plants can leave his sheep paralyzed or very ill. The shepherd goes ahead to eradicate them.

- *Predators*—The shepherd will look for signs of wolves, coyotes, cougars, and bears. He takes great pains to trap them so they cannot harm the sheep.

- *Adders*—These small brown snakes live underground. They pop out of their holes and bite the noses of grazing sheep. Their bite infects, and sometimes even kills the sheep. The shepherd pours a circle of oil around the hole. Adders are repulsed by the smell of the oil, so the sheep can safely graze.

- *Dangerous drinking places*—The shepherd clears the debris, twigs, stones, and soil that have fallen into the water source. He also builds small dams or repairs those he has already made to hold the still waters. That is all part of his work to prepare the table for the sheep.

Don't Miss the Prepared Feast

The Shepherd has prepared a table before us, and it is grand and abundant. The enemies are still present, but the Good Shepherd doesn't bring us this far to abandon us. During times when our circumstances are beyond our control and our enemy seems to loom over us, we need to turn our eyes on the Lord.

After the shepherd brings the sheep through the dangerous valley, the enemy may be present, but the shepherd will not permit him to come to the table. (File that away for later.)

Sometimes we miss the prepared table because of our enemies. And what a shame for us. Sometimes our enemies seem larger and more prevalent than the table that has been prepared. I've been guilty of seeing the enemy instead of the table. Have you?

With the ordeal of the valley behind the sheep, a glorious luscious feast awaits them. Philip Keller tells us when the sheep get a glimpse of this beautiful grassy tableland, they run with excitement. Why?

- It is a lush table of abundance.
- It is a lush table of provision.
- It is a lush table of perfect communion.
- It is a lush table of fellowship prepared by the "Good Shepherd Himself."

Have you ever gone through a valley experience and later came to realize it was a blessing? Did you come to understand that the Lord was with you and was blessing you through the darkest places? This passage comes to mind:

For you, O God, have tested us; you have tried us as silver is tried. You brought us into the net; you laid a crushing burden on our backs; you let men ride over our heads; we went through the fire and through water; yet you have brought us out to a place of abundance (Psalm 66:10–12 ESV).

The following pastoral word pictures, indelibly planted in your mind from the verses above, will bring you incessant joy and deep comfort in times of trouble.

- You have gone through the roughest, darkest terrain, but you get a view of the green grass that you have waited for so patiently.

- You've gone through fire, you've gone through deep waters, and now you've come to a lush table prepared just for you.

- You are excited as you see what's ahead. You start to run because you're headed to a table that has been prepared.

> *We went through the fire and through water; yet you have brought us out to a place of abundance.*
>
> **—Psalm 66:12**

Oh, taste and see that the Lord is good. Blessed is the man [the Shepherd's daughter] who takes refuge in him (Psalm 34:8 ESV).

Focus on Jesus, the Good Shepherd

We humans, as the sheep of His pasture, should be aware of the dangers and enemies that surround us.

- The appetites of our own flesh
- The enemy we fight in our minds
- People who oppose God
- Sin or tragedy in our past
- A spouse who doesn't know the Lord
- Sickness
- Death
- Fear
- Depression
- Anxiety

How do we combat these enemies? By refusing to concentrate on the invaders, but instead, keeping the Shepherd in the limelight. Isn't it comforting to know that, as a shepherd prepares a green luscious table for his flock, our Good Shepherd has gone ahead and prepared a table for us?

We do have the tendency to spotlight the wrong things, don't we? Why not begin to target glorious things? Our Lord has already dealt our archenemy a striking blow. Do you really believe that? Do you believe it enough to find comfort in that fact?

The Fatal Blow

Genesis 3:15 describes what the coming of the Lord will do to our adversary, Satan, who planned to bring us death. But Jesus defeated him through His death and resurrection.

> Concerning His Son Jesus Christ our Lord, who was born of the seed of David according to the flesh, and declared to be the Son of God with power according to the Spirit of holiness, by the resurrection from the dead (Romans 1:3–4).

> And if Christ is not risen, your faith is futile; you are still in your sins (1 Corinthians 15:17)!

> Knowing that Christ, having been raised from the dead, dies no more. Death no longer has dominion over Him (Romans 6:9).

Jesus is the firstborn from the dead, meaning, He will never die again (Colossians 1:18). Jesus has resurrection power, and because of Him, so do we. Satan must have thought he had dealt the final blow in this age-old war of sin and death. What was the devil's grave miscalculation? The cross was heaven's triumph. So when Jesus Christ arose, the power of sin and death were forever shattered. Because of the resurrection, the presence of Satan cannot have power over Christ. And Christians have no reason to listen to the adversary, even though he walks about like a roaring lion (1 Peter 5:8). Because of Jesus' death and resurrection, we can resist the devil and be assured the thief's power pales in comparison to our powerful God. We can have faith and confidence that that we will not be overcome because Jesus has already won the victory.

> I'm not afraid of the devil. The devil can handle me—he's got judo I never heard of. But he can't handle the One to whom I'm joined; he can't handle the One to whom I'm united; he can't handle the One whose nature dwells in my nature.[21]
>
> —A. W. Tozer

Abundant Life *Zoē*

Don't focus on the enemy, focus on the Shepherd. He has invited us to come to the table, and it is ready for a feast. Jesus said, "The thief does not come except to steal, and to kill, and to destroy. I have come that they may have life, and that they may have it more abundantly" (John 10:10).

There are two words used for *life* in the scriptures: *bios*, meaning breath in your lungs, physical life; and *zoē*, meaning full, exuberant, extraordinary life, the fullness of life beyond the physical. The word Jesus used is *zoē*.

Zoē life is used 135 times in the Bible compared to *bios* life, which is used only 10 times. Why do you think *zoē* life is used 125 times more than *bios* life? Should we be more focused on the abundant life the Good Shepherd offers rather than on our physical circumstances?

Think of it this way. Our table is always prepared, but the enemy of our soul is always present. Agreed? That enemy strategizes day and night to get us to focus on and settle for the *bios* life. If we do that, we will never taste the hell-shattering goodness of *zoē* life. So what

Don't focus on the enemy, focus on the Shepherd.

---

21 "Top 25 Inspirational Christian Quotes," ChristianQuotes.com. Accessed August 1, 2019. https://www.christianquotes.info/top-quotes/top-25-inspirational-quotes/#ixzz5It1DHPrC.

causes us to forfeit the *zoē* life for the *bios* life? Since the table is furnished abundantly, how do we fail to see it? Our vision is out of focus.

The *zoē* life is the satisfied life. It can be here and now. Our Shepherd didn't give His life for the sheep in order for them to just exist. He gave it so we could experience the high summer range of a thriving abundant life in Him. Our Good Shepherd is immensely pleased to see us flourish on the table-lands He has made possible.

Tables of Intentionality

During the years of my dad's care, there were so many tables of abundance that the Lord provided, and I came to understand the purpose of intentionality. By this I mean seeing the blessing in the presence of my circumstances. I had come to understand that Dad wasn't going to get better, but I did have some time to spend with him. I tried to see the good and face the bad in stride. Sometimes I did okay. At other times I made a complete mess of everything. But when I intended to see the good, on purpose, I found that I captured a wonderful feast of blessings.

Here are some examples:

- Conversations with my dad, those little windows into his soul when he shared his life with me.
- Afternoon drives and ice cream cones.
- Avenues of service, for both Dad and other residents in the assisted living home.
- Mother-daughter time with Anna, our youngest, as we traveled several times each week to visit Dad.
- Sister-talks about Dad's condition.
- Humorous stories that unfolded while Anna and I visited Dad.

Now I think back on these times, and I see that the Lord had gone ahead and prepared a table for me, and yes, even in the presence of my enemy. And that helps me to be intentional in seeing His table in subsequent trials.

136

What opposition did I have during those days? I was exhausted and frustrated because it seemed I never had the time to do what I needed to do. I felt overwhelmed and angered by things out of my control. And yet, as those enemy forces were at work, the Lord was preparing a table for me. I just didn't realize it at the time.

- What are ways that you can miss the table that has been prepared for you?

- How is intentionality an important part of seeing the table instead of the enemy?

- How do you see the enemy at work in 2 Corinthians 4:8–10? And our Shepherd in verse 14?

> Our own table will never be as abundant as the one He has prepared for us.

Our Shepherd ensures us that we can enjoy gladness with our sadness and have sunshine in the midst of the shadow. We can't create that kind of tranquility, and our own table will never be as abundant as the one He has prepared for us.

Oh, the benefits of being the Shepherd's daughter!

Sheep Homework

1. Recite the Twenty-third Psalm and add, "Oh, the benefits of being the Shepherd's daughter."

2. Memorize John 10:10.

3. Invite someone to your table this week.

4. Notice the tables of abundance around you.

5. Focus on the Shepherd instead of the enemy.

6. Be intentional and notice some of the tables He has prepared, and record them.

7. Are you living the *zoē* life or the *bios* life?

Note: See Appendix pages 185 through 194 for a deeper study of His "table."

A Fly
In My Ointment

Recite the Twenty-third Psalm.
At the end, add, "Oh, the benefits of being the Shepherd's daughter."

n the terminology of a sheepman, summertime is fly time. Hot weather is the worst time for sheep. The summer months can be sheer torture if they aren't protected. Fleas and ticks are on the attack, causing sheep to itch and scratch. These pesky insects can cause the skin to become infected and inflamed.

But while fleas and ticks abound, the worst pest for sheep is the nasal fly—the botfly. These flies buzz around the sheep's head attempting to deposit their eggs in the damp muscuous membrane of the sheep's nose. If they are successful, the eggs will hatch in a few days and work their way up the nasal cavity and into the head of the sheep. They burrow into the flesh and set up an intense irritation inside the sheep's head. Severe inflamation usually follows.

If left untreated, the sheep, in search of relief, look for large rocks, fence posts, or anything they can beat or bang their heads against. They will do whatever they can to find temporary relief from the torture. In extreme cases the sheep go blind. Some will even kill themselves by repeatedly beating their heads. Thus the term "beating your brains out."

When these flies invade the flock, the sheep become nervous and afraid. They seem to know what the flies can do to them, so they become frantic, running back and forth trying to escape. They sometimes run themselves to exhaustion. Ewes start losing weight, stop milking their lambs, and stop growing because they become panicked and anxious.

Do you see any parallels between sheep that are bugged and our own behavior during a crisis or an aggravating situation?

I Want to Beat My Brains Out

What bugs you? What puts your nerves on edge?

- The scraping of fingernails on a chalkboard?
- A tissue left in a shirt pocket that has spread bits and pieces to all other clothes in in the washing machine?
- Slow drivers when you're in a hurry?
- People with annoying habits?
- A family member who creates problems?

Could our fly be a besetting sin that's hard to overcome? What about the sins of others who cause us pain, disappointment, and heartache? Where's the ointment?

 List some flies that annoy you.

 Describe the parallels between sheep and humans when we are "bugged."

 How does sin infect us?

Describe how sin can cause so much damage in our lives and for others.

Most Americans grew up hearing and using common expressions about flies:

- "I'd like to be a fly on the wall."
- "She wouldn't hurt a fly."
- "They are dropping like flies!"
- "There is a fly in the ointment!"

Most of us know all too well about flies in the ointment and our response to them. I wish I could tell you that I always respond to negatives like the perfect "church lady," but that's not the case. Sometimes things just bug me. When I feel "bugged" by circumstances out of my control, it's time to apply that special ointment to the place the "botfly" wants to trespass. Thank God it works!

The Answer Is in the Oil

He anoints our heads with oil while we are dealing with our enemies.

The sheep still have flies all around them, don't they? Of course they do, but the shepherd is protecting his flock. He meets their needs even while the enemy buzzes around their heads. Only the shepherd can provide that kind of protection.

Philip Keller writes:

I always preferred to use a homemade remedy composed of linseed oil, sulphur, and tar which was smeared over the sheep's nose and head as a protection against nose flies. Once the oil had been applied to the sheep's head there was an immediate change in behaviour.[22]

The shepherd's anointing is a perfect picture of our Good Shepherd protecting and caring for us, even in the presence of the enemy. He is the gracious

---

22 Keller, *A Shepherd Looks at Psalm 23*, 116.

> We need always to be keenly aware that we can yield to our irritations or we can yield to Him.

host of the tableland, and He will handle any cares and concerns His sheep may face.

Gone are the irritations. Gone are the frenzy, restlessness, and anxiousness. Gone are the aggravations and irritability when His oil is applied.When we begin to feel bugged by a difficult situation or by those petty annoyances that torment us to the point of wanting to beat our brains out, it is time to turn to the one who can bring relief. The enemies we face are spiritual and much more threatening than the enemies that confront sheep.

One application of the oil was not enough for the sheep to forestall the flies. There must be a continual application throughout the summer months.

So it is with the Shepherd's daughters. We must continually turn to the fresh oil applications of His Word and Spirit. Our Master, Christ Himself, urges us to ask for the help given to us by the Father (Luke 11:13).

Ask the Savior to Help You

Just as the shepherd regularly applies the oil to the sheep in a pasture, when we belong to Him, He continuously helps us. If our prayers seem feeble, they won't be when they reach His throne, because His Spirit makes intercession for us (Romans 8:26).

As we read and meditate on God's Word, His gracious guidance brings healing, comfort, and relief from the frustrations of life. When a problem seems to be too much for us to endure, we need to give it to Him: "Father, this is beyond me. I can't cope with it. It's bugging me. I can't rest, so please take over."

We need always to be keenly aware that we can yield to our irritations or we can yield to Him. Throughout the New Testament, we are given examples of what goes on inside the child of God when we want to yield to ungodly behavior. It is as if there is a tug of war going on inside the mind. It's a battle you can't afford to lose, so stay close to the Shepherd and He will protect you.

Which Realm Do You Choose? Life or Death?

The botfly does not necessarily lead to physical death for sheep; there is a cure. But as the Good Shepherd's sheep, we as Shepherd's daughters, make the choice for the cure.

Two realms are described in the scriptures: the realm of the flesh and the realm of the Spirit. Let's consider them.

- *When we follow the flesh, we allow our mind to be controlled by our impulses and desires.* We allow sin to take over and bring harm to us and our relationships, as the sheep are bugged by the flies, causing them to behave and act in ways that bring harm to themselves.

- *When we follow the Spirit, we choose to yield to His righteousness and we desire to please God.* We are enabled by a knowledge of the Spirit's revelation to live and behave differently from those who do not know Christ. That brings life and harmony to us, just as oil brings relief to tortured sheep.

Read Romans 8:5–16. In which realm are you living, the flesh or the Spirit?

What is the difference in being led by the flesh and led by the Spirit?

To which one must we yield if we are His?

What happens when we allow our flesh to direct us? Describe spiritual death.

How would yielding to the Spirit help the annoyances in our lives?

How do we allow ourselves to yield to His direction when we are feeling "bugged"? Why must we make an intentional effort?

As Christians, we must be led by God's Word given by His Spirit. If we choose to be led by our fleshly desires, we are lusting against the Spirit.

> I say then: Walk in the Spirit, and you shall not fulfill the lust of the flesh. For the flesh lusts against the Spirit, and the Spirit against the flesh; and these are contrary to one another, so that you do not do the things that you wish. Now the works of the flesh are evident, which are: adultery, fornication, uncleanness, lewdness, idolatry, sorcery, hatred, contentions, jealousies, outbursts of wrath, selfish ambitions, dissensions, heresies, envy, murders, drunkenness, revelries, and the like; of which I tell you beforehand, just as I also told you in time past, that those who practice such things will not inherit the kingdom of God (Galatians 5:16–21).

Get Out of Dysfunction Junction

When we allow our flesh to rule our lives, then we turn down the street to that ever-so-popular area I call *Dysfunction Junction.* When we enter Dysfunction Junction, we allow the "flies" of anger, frustration, negativity, and all kinds of sinful behavior to overtake us. This is a place where confusion, angry hearts, hateful looks, and unwholesome words reside. This is the place where relationships go to die.

Dysfunction Junction is not the place for the Shepherd's daughter. Our Shepherd leads His sheep "in the paths of righteousness for His name's sake." We don't have to live with the pests of Dysfunction Junction when we have the healing oil from our Shepherd. He is in control.

 Why is Dysfunction Junction no place for the Shepherd's daughter?

 Make a list of harmful "flies" that live there.

How are Christians supposed to be different?

What can you do to get out of Dysfunction Junction?

Read Romans 8:26–27. What does the Holy Spirit provide for the Shepherd's daughter?

How do these verses help you to understand that you have Divine help with every situation in your life?

When we are bugged, we don't have to act like those who don't know God. We have the revelation of His Spirit, the Bible. Follow its guidance and be set free from Dysfunction Junction.

Since we have the Holy Spirit's written revelation to study and meditate upon, and we have access to the Father through prayer with a guarantee that the Holy Spririt will intercede for us (Romans 8:26), God has made a way to control the flies that torment us. We do not have to live in Dysfunction Junction.

Where Is My Oil?

Do you believe the promise of the scriptures for daily healing oil? Not old rancid oil, but fresh pure oil, was God's choice for exalting the psalmist:

> But my horn You have exalted like a wild ox; I have been anointed with fresh oil. My eye also has seen my desire on my enemies; My ears hear my desire on the wicked who rise up against me (Psalm 92:10–11).

Why do we often miss out on the reviving oil of our Good Shepherd? Jesus instructed:

> Ask, and it will be given to you; seek, and you will find; knock, and it will be opened to you. For everyone who asks receives, and he who seeks finds, and to him who knocks it will be opened (Luke 11:9–10).

> No matter
> what causes
> us to want
> to beat our
> brains out,
> we must
> return to the
> Lord and ask
> for His help.

This is how we know He will continue to sustain us with the healing oil for our daily flies. We just have to ask. I believe what the scripture promises.

I want you to know this "church lady" has learned to ask the Lord for my fresh oil every morning. So many times in my life I allowed my flesh to take control, even though I belonged to Christ. I do not want to leave the impression that I have mastered the flesh. That would mean that I am perfect, and I am not. But I have learned to go quickly to my Shepherd and ask for His help when my flesh wants to rule and when the flies appear. It is during these times that I ask the Lord for help to see His healing oil.

No matter what irritates us or causes us to want to beat our brains out, we must return to the Lord and ask for His help. Why should we keep asking for it? Because He told us to keep asking. He has promised that His Spirit is pleading for me. I must trust His deliverance.

Crucify the Flesh to Walk in the Spirit

The flies are still around us. However, they cannot infect us if the oil is applied. When the oil is applied, rest, peace, and self-control are evident in our lives. Since, His word dwells in us if we belong to Him, and we are controlled by His Spirit. We can choose a life filled with joy unspeakable.

> But the fruit of the Spirit is love, joy, peace, longsuffering, kindness, good-ness, faithfulness, gentleness, self-control. Against such there is no law. And those who are Christ's have crucified the flesh with its passions and desires. If we live in the Spirit, let us also walk in the Spirit (Galatians 5:22–25).

 If we live by the Spirit, to whom do we belong?

According to Galatians 5:22–25, what nine characteristics does the Spirit produce in us?

Is it possible to produce the fruit of the Spirit without Him or His Word? Defend your answer.

How are we to walk?

The word *fruit* is singular in Galatians 5. There is one fruit with nine different characteristics. Let's do an exercise.

Imagine that I am in front of you holding an apple. If I ask you to describe the apple, giving nine different characteristics, how would you do that? Would you mention leaves, color, taste, shape, size, texture, spotted, plain, and classification (Red Delicious, Golden, Fuji)? If you mentioned these or others, you described one "fruit" or "apple" with several characteristics.

In a similar way, the key to understanding the "fruit of the Spirit" is found in the two verses that follow. We cannot stop at verse 23, as many often do. Paul connects these charaertistics with something very important.

> And those who are Christ's have crucified the flesh with its passions and desires. If we live in the Spirit, let us also walk in the Spirit (Galatians 5:24–25).

In order for the Spirit to produce the fruit, what must we crucify?

What has happened to our flesh if we are His?

How do we live in the Spirit? Is this a daily practice?

How do we walk by the Spirit? Is this a daily practice?

Dear one, in order to possess the nine characteristics of the Spirit, we must crucify our flesh. That means we will make a conscience effort to overcome anything that impedes us spiritually. It is a daily practice. It will take diligence and patience on our part. Does that mean we will be perfect, that we will never make a mistake? Of course not. But it does mean that we have stepped over into a different way of life. It means we surrender to Him, and we no longer live for our own selfish desires, but now we live to please Him. Then when those annoying flies come our way, we can ask Him to give us His love, peace, goodness, and kindness as we deal with difficulties.

The Shepherd's daughter lives in freedom, love, and kindness. She is more concerned with her character than with outward beauty. She is not easily annoyed or frustrated. In fact, "her worth is far above rubies. . . . Many daughters have done well, but you excel them all" (Proverbs 31:10, 29).

- I'm not good on my own, but I know the One who is.
- I can't produce my own peace, but I know Who can.
- I'm not kind on my own, but I know one Who is.
- I do not have self-control on my own, but I know Who does.

When we put our cares in His hand, He puts His peace in our hearts.
—Tim Gustafson

Oh, the benefits of being the Shepherd's daughter!

Sheep Homework

1. Spend time this week identifying what areas of your flesh keep you in Dysfunction Junction.

2. Memorize Romans 8:26–27.

3. Since He helps us in our weaknesses, what weakness do you need to yield to Him?

4. How can you help others live by the Spirit and not by the flesh.

5. Realize that the nine characteristics of the Spirit describe one fruit.

6. Why is it impossible to have self-control without love or peace?

7. Why is patience necessary for kindness and goodness?

8. How can you share this lesson with someone else?

9. Write the benefits of being the Shepherd's daughter.

12

My
Overflowing Cup

My Cup Runs Over

Recite the Twenty-third Psalm.

At the end, add, "Oh, the benefits of being the Shepherd's daughter."

The pessimist says, my cup is half empty. The optimist says, my cup is half full. The Shepherd's daughter says, "My cup runs over!"

When you think of the brim of a cup, you are considering the highest point the cup can be filled without overflowing. David gives us a word picture in Psalm 23:5: "My cup runs over."

At this point of the psalm, summer is moving into autumn. It is a restful time as the bright green landscape turns golden. The sheep have a respite from the tormenting insects. No other season finds the flock so contented, fit, and strong. No wonder David penned, "My cup runs over."

Every time I think of the overflowing cup, my mind immediately goes to Niagara Falls. The water flows continuously, running over the falls, flowing steadily. Each time I go to the falls, I think about Psalm 23:5. That's the idea David is trying to give us in this four-word thought.

Our Good Shepherd is not a stingy host. He never gives sparingly and, as a sheep under His care, we can easily say: "What more could I want or desire?"

The Sheep's Cup of Blessings

What is the meaning of "my cup overflows" concerning the sheep? Since it is autumn, the shepherd begins to drive the sheep back to the pastures of home. When the weather begins to freeze, they can become so chilled that they cannot move, and if they lie down in the cold, they become cramped.

This is a time when the shepherd has to give them a special "medicine"—wine. The wine makes them feel warm and enables them to move slowly homeward.

Philip Keller writes that during these times he carried a mixture of brandy and water in his pocket. When a ewe lamb became chilled from the wet cold weather, he would pour a few spoonfuls down her throat. In a matter of minutes, she had renewed energy. It has been said that the sheep actually wiggle their tails in excitement as the brandy warms their chilled bodies.

The Wine of His Blood

What a picture for us as Jesus, our Good Shepherd, shares the wine of His blood poured out at Calvary

> But at the same time, unexpected blizzards can blow up or sleet storms suddenly shroud the hills. The flock and the owner can pass through appalling suffering together. It is here that I grasp another meaning of a cup that overflows. There is in every life a cup of suffering. Jesus Christ referred to His agony in the Garden of Gethsemane and at Calvary as His cup. And had it not overflowed with His life poured out for men, we would have perished.[23]

> This wine is my blood, which will be poured out to forgive the sins of many and begin the new agreement from God to his people (Matthew 26:28 ERV).

---

23 Keller, *A Shepherd Looks at Psalm 23*, 125.

My Cup Is Dry

When trials and long periods of stress and anxiety seem to capture us, we are often prone, like sheep, to wander off the path. When sheep wander, it is usually because they are discontented. As the sheep of the Good Shepherd, we need to remind ourselves constantly that His blood has overflowed to us and that He constantly pours His blessings on us.

Life's problems sometimes make us feel drained, empty, and lifeless. Why do we often feel like the pessimist whose cup is half empty?

During Dad's illness I sometimes forgot to count my blessings. In the midst of doctors, sickness, and depression, and as Dad's body was failing him, it was hard to keep the proper perspective. Dad was usually a positive person, but during this time, he began to see his life as half empty, and I could understand why.

These are some reasons he felt half empty:

- He was wheelchair-bound.
- He was homesick, in assisted living.
- He had restricted activity.
- He had to depend on others for his needs and wants.
- He was lonely.
- He suffered daily health struggles (blood pressure, no energy, nervousness).

Because his cup felt dry, so did mine. Has that ever happened to you? Probably. When a loved one begins to suffer with a chronic illness and struggle with life's inevitable changes, those difficulties begin to trickle down. It was during this time that I started counting everyday blessings. It was a season when I learned that God was still there, overloading me with His benefits. But I had to consciously look for them every day. As God's children, we must determine why we are pessimistic and then focus on our blessings daily.

Count Your Blessings, Not Your Troubles

When faced with difficulties, it is not easy to see the good in our lives. We allow our attitudes and thoughts to become clouded by our circumstances, and if we aren't careful, negativity sets in. Let's look at some verses in the book of Psalms.

- Psalm 68:19: "Blessed be the Lord who daily loads us with benefits." "Daily loads us with benefits?" That means every day, all day long, those benefits keep coming.

- Psalm 103:2: "Bless the Lord, O my soul, and forget not all His benefits." According to this verse, there is a possibility of forgetting His blessings. How do we prevent that from happening to us?

- Psalm 116:12: "What shall I render to the Lord for all His benefits to me?" How should we praise the Lord for all of His benefits? How often should we thank Him?

- Psalm 116:13: "I will take up the cup of salvation, and call upon the name of the Lord." In this psalm, David writes of the pains of death, trouble, and sorrow (v. 3). He writes of being delivered from death, tears, and falling (v. 8). He talks of great afflictions (v. 10).

David shares real-life experiences with us. As we read this psalm, it is easy to identify with many of the experiences David mentions. The idea is that no matter the situation, we are blessed by the Lord.

Understanding Our Cup of Blessings

Paul understood an overflowing cup of blessings when he wrote his words of comfort and assurance in Philippians 4:13. He basically says, "I have plenty. I am well-supplied. In any and all circumstances my strength comes from Jesus Himself." Paul is giving us the idea behind "my cup overflows." How could he say that when awaiting death?

Like Paul writing Philippians, write your blessings during your times of difficulty.

Paul knew something deeper. He knew that his joy and abundance were still flowing, regardless of his circumstances. He realized who supplied what he needed, and he was full of joy.

Paul understood that our worth, overflowing peace, confidence, and joy come to us as His sheep through His cup of suffering turned blessing for us.

We see throughout the scriptures the idea of "my cup overflows." And there is a reason: When you know the Good Shepherd, your cup will always overflow. The cup isn't big enough to hold all of the blessings from the Lord.

 List a few of the spiritual blessings you enjoy in Christ.

How Large Is Your Heart?

Your heart is the cup. Is your heart large enough to hold the blessings He wants to give to you? He keeps pouring so many blessings into your life that they literally flow over the edge of the cup. As the cup overflows, the blessings run all over the table and stream down onto the floor. They flow underneath the doorway, out into the yard, and down the sidewalk. And guess what? They keep coming. The flow is continuous. It never stops.

I think of Peter when Jesus was washing His feet. At first Peter was confused and didn't want the Lord to wash his feet. When Peter finally understood what the Lord was doing, he said, "Lord, not my feet only, but also my hands and my head" (John 13:9).

Adopt Peter's Attitude

This should be the words of every Shepherd's daughter: "Lord, pour Your blessings upon me. Let them flow as steadily as a beautiful fountain. But Lord, please let me count the blessings and become mindful of them every single day. Thank You for Your love, mercy, forgiveness, and goodness. Thank You for opening a continuous flowing fountain of blessings in my life. Let me live in an attitude of gratitude like Paul."

F. B. Myer penned these words long ago:

> Whatever blessing is in our cup, it is sure to run over. With Him the calf is always the fatted calf; the robe is always the best robe; the joy is unspeakable; the peace passeth understanding . . . There is no grudging in God's benevolence; He does not measure out His goodness as an apothecary counts his drops and measures his drams, slowly and exactly, drop by drop. God's way is always characterized by multitudinous and overflowing bounty.[24]

Summer's Over

It is now time for the sheep to begin to follow the shepherd as he starts toward home. Autumn has arrived. Storms and early snow have begun to sweep over the high country.

As the sheep start home, it is a time when they are free to rest. The flies of the summer season are gone, as well as the other annoying insects. No other time finds the sheep so full of life and strong. No wonder David penned: "My cup overflows."

Consider these scriptures in light of an overflowing cup:

- John 7:38: "He who believes in Me, as the Scripture has said, out of his heart will flow rivers of living water." *What flows from the cup?*

- John 10:10: "I have come that they may have life, and that they may have it more abundantly." *What flows from the cup?*

- Ephesians 1:3: "Blessed be the God and Father of our Lord Jesus Christ, who has blessed us with every spiritual blessing in the heavenly places in Christ." *What flows from the cup?*

Do you get a sense that the scripture is telling you not to look at life with a pessimistic nature? The scripture tells us to look at our cup as full and

---

24 F. B. Myer, *Shepherd Psalm* (CreateSpace Independent Publishing, 2017; first published in 1895), 96.

overflowing. Count your blessings, because no matter what problems you may be facing, it will always be true that you have more blessings than problems. That's a divine promise to us as His children.

We serve a God who is rich in mercy and a God who willingly pardons us. How do I know? Listen to the verse: "Where sin increased, grace abounded all the more" (Romans 5:20 ESV). His grace overflows beyond your sins!

This is what we must understand about the overflowing cup: We follow a Shepherd who can bless us and provide continuous grace no matter our circumstances or how enormous we feel our sins to be.

Don't Live Out of a Half-Empty Cup

Christians often do that, you know. We become negative and begin to complain. We find fault with other people and tear one another down. We are low on love. When we so live as Christians, we aren't living from an overflowing cup, and it shows on our faces.

What should be our countenance as His sheep? We have benefits, remember! Those blessings should be stored in our hearts and displayed on our faces. We should have a bubbling fountain deep within us.

We are the billboard for God. When people look at us, they should see the most joyful contented people on earth. We are supposed to be the happiest people because we know the Lord. We have an overflowing cup. Let people see it.

Got Religion

A story is told of a little girl who visited her grandfather's farm. Her grandfather was a Christian. As he began to show her his animals, the little girl observed them carefully.

They went first to the chicken yard and saw all the chickens scratching and pecking in the newly mowed grass. She said, "Well, the chickens ain't got it." The grandfather thought, "Ain't got what?"

Then they went to a corral where a young colt was running and kicking up his hooves. She said to her grandpa, "Well, he ain't got it."

Next she saw a cow grazing, moving her lower jaw as she chewed. "She ain't got it either," she said.

Finally she went into the barn and saw this long-faced, droopy-eared donkey. "Grandpa," she said excitedly, "he's got it, he's got it, he's got it!"

"He's got what, my dear?" the grandpa asked.

"Religion!" she replied. "He's got religion! He looks like you!"

Does our countenance portray a picture of a sheep in His care or does it say to others that we are just skimping by, barely surviving? Our picture should be of one who is blessed with a continuous flowing fountain of blessings. In the Lord's presence and care, there is abundance and fullness. We need to show others that we have a cup that never runs dry.

Jesus Opened the Overflowing Cup

Jesus' death on the cross occurred at the ninth hour. The earth quaked. And at His resurrection, graves were open and the dead came forth and walked around. You might say, the fountain was just opened (Matthew 27:46–53).

John records that the soldiers broke the legs of the two criminals crucified with Him. This was to hasten their deaths. As the soldiers approached Jesus, they noticed that He was already dead. Then one soldier took a spear and pierced His side, and immediately blood and water came out of His body. Again, the fountain was opened even further, in fact to overflowing (John 19:31–37).

Little did the soldiers know that as they pierced His side, He was opening a fountain that would continuously flow to all who believe and obey Him. Is it any wonder that His sheep can make the claim: My cup runs over?

And He said to me, "It is done! I am the Alpha and the Omega, the Beginning and the End. I will give of the fountain of the water of life freely to him who thirsts" (Revelation 21:6).

The Lord will guide you continually, and satisfy your soul in drought, and strengthen your bones; you shall be like a watered garden, and like a spring of water, whose waters do not fail (Isaiah 58:11).

We may feel as though we are living in a parched and dry land, but for those who follow the Good Shepherd, their land will never be parched. It will never be dry. In fact, it will be flowing like a fountain that's running over the brim. Oh, the benefits of being the Shepherd's daughter!

Drinking from My Saucer

I've never made a fortune, and it's probably too late now.
But I don't worry about that much, I'm happy anyhow.
And as I go along life's way, I'm reaping better than I sowed.
I'm drinking from my saucer, 'cause my cup has overflowed.
I don't have a lot of riches, and sometimes the going's tough.
But I've got loved ones around me, and that makes me rich
    enough.
I thank God for His blessings, and the mercies He's bestowed.
I'm drinking from my saucer, 'cause my cup has overflowed.
I remember times when things went wrong, my faith wore
    somewhat thin.
But all at once the dark clouds broke, and the sun peeped through
    again.
So God, help me not to gripe about the tough rows I've hoed.
I'm drinking from my saucer, 'cause my cup has overflowed.
If God gives me strength and courage, when the way grows steep
    and rough.
I'll not ask for other blessings, I'm already blessed enough.
And may I never be too busy, to help others bear their loads.
Then I'll keep drinking from my saucer, 'cause my cup has
    overflowed.[25]

—John Paul Moore

---

25 John Paul Moore, *All Worship Blog*, posted September 9, 2014, https://www.allworship.com
/drinking-saucer/.

When you are the Shepherd's daughter, you'll always be drinking from your saucer.

Oh the benefits of being the Shepherd's daughter!

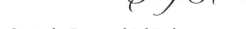

Sheep Homework

1. Quote the Twenty-third Psalm.

2. By now, you should be able to name the benefits of each verse. Recite the psalm and after each verse, say the benefits.

3. Memorize Isaiah 58:11.

4. Study the last day in the life of Jesus. Read each gospel account of His death, and notice the ways He opened an overflowing cup of blessings to us.

5. Remember to keep drinking from your saucer.

13

Two Bodyguards

Goodness and Mercy Shall Follow Me

Recite the Twenty-third Psalm.

At the end, add, "Oh, the benefits of being the Shepherd's daughter."

One of the benefits of having bodyguards is that they are with you every hour of every day. They follow you wherever you go. If you go to the mall, they are there. If you go to a friend's house, they are still with you. When you're in the shower or you're taking a nap, your bodyguards are standing outside the door. The idea is that they are always following the person they are guarding.

Now let us turn our attention to one of the most beautiful verses in the psalm: "Surely goodness and mercy shall follow me all the days of my life." His goodness and mercy pursue us. It's as if they are tracking us down. These are like jewels in a treasure box for the child of God.

These words stand to remind us on our darkest days that there is still goodness and mercy to be found. When does His "goodness and mercy" follow me? All the days of my life! All means everyday, all day long. His goodness and mercy are pursuing me.

- When I'm asleep
- When I'm at work
- When I'm resting or digging in the dirt
- When I'm having lunch with my friends
- When I'm standing by the bedside of a loved one
- When I'm _____
  (you fill in the blank)

> As I see in retrospect I realize that for the one who is truly in Christ care, no difficulty can arise, no dilemma emerge, no seeming disaster descend on the life without eventual good coming out of the chaos. This is to see the goodness and mercy of my Master in my life. It has become the great foundation of my faith and confidence in Him.[26]

What Does That Verse Mean?

Surely means "certain, absolute, non-negotiable, without a doubt." That means there is no guessing, no wondering, and no question marks.

We live in a world that is ever-changing, and that means nothing is certain. For example, our moods often shift. We might be happy one minute and depressed the next. We might even change our mind.

When we are asked, "Are you sure about that?" we might say, "Well, I thought I was sure, but now I'm not so sure." People we love can stop loving us. The world as we know it can change in a moment's notice. Many times, because we live in an uncertain world, we feel uncertain about life. But not the Shepherd's daughters. Oh no! We know something different.

David doesn't say maybe, possibly, or I have a hunch that His goodness and mercy will follow me. David writes as a sheep boasting with confidence. God doesn't change His mood, mind, or promises. He is a sure God. Paul says

---

26 Keller, *A Shepherd Looks at Psalm 23*, 129.

in 2 Timothy 2:13, "If we are faithless, He remains faithful; He cannot deny Himself."

The very essence of God is that He is faithful, and He can be no other way toward His children.

What does the faithfulness of God mean to you?

Read Hebrews 13:8. How does this verse comfort you in an ever-changing world?

Goodness means "kind, profitable, the beneficial quality of something." God's goodness to us is for our benefit. It is profitable even when things seem not so good.

Read Psalm 52:1. How long does God's goodness endure?

Read Titus 3:4–7. What does "being an heir according to the hope of eternal life" do for us spiritually according to verses 4–6? Explain how this is poured out upon us?

Mercy means "withholding of the punishment or judgment we deserve." When I think of mercy, I think of the gift of Jesus Christ and the love that God had for us. Jesus took our sins to the cross so we could receive God's forgiveness instead of the wrath and judgment we deserved. God did not and will not punish us because Jesus has paid the price. That's mercy.

Read Ephesians 2:4–5. Why is God so rich in mercy?

Read 2 Samuel 24:14. What is the difference in God's mercy and man's mercy?

What does David tell us about the mercies of God? If the Lord is the Shepherd who leads the flock, goodness and mercy are like two bodyguards that guard the rear of the flock. Not just goodness alone, because we are sinners in need of mercy. Not just mercy alone, because we are fragile creatures in need of goodness. We need them both. As one man wrote, "Goodness to supply every want and mercy to forgive every sin. Goodness to provide. Mercy to pardon."

Follow in Hebrew is *radaph*: "to pursue; to set off after someone in order to catch them." We think of God as enthroned in heaven, in one place. But David gives us a picture of a God who follows, pursues, and chases us. You need not go further than Genesis 3 to find God in the role of a seeker. Genesis 3:9 says, "Where are you?" With that question God began a quest to seek the human heart.

All the days of my life. What a huge statement. Look at the size of it. It is a sure and certain thing that goodness and mercy will follow the child of God every day! Think of the things that fill the days ahead of you.

- Days at home with a toddler? *He is at your side.*

- Days in a seemingly dead-end job? *His goodness and mercy are there to walk with you.*

- Days of loneliness and sadness? *He is there to take your hand.*

Surely goodness and mercy shall follow me—not some, not most, not a few, but all—all the days of my life.

Undeserved Mercy in Hard Times

Can you boldly make the claim that God's goodness and mercy have followed you all the days of your life? I pray so because this is the only claim the Shepherd's daughter can make.

You may say, "Now wait a minute, Debbie. I have been through many situations that were not so pleasant. I can't say for certain that God's goodness and mercy were following me at times."

If you are saying these things, I understand your thought process. But as reflecting sheep, we can't miss His goodness and mercy, because it has been there. Following. Pursuing. When the sheep in the psalm makes this claim, it is somewhat of a boast and an exclamation of confidence in the one who controls his destiny.

You may have experienced the blessings of goodness and mercy in spite of the following:

- Your presence at the bedside of a loved one was not enough to stop or numb the pain or keep death at bay.

- Your job folded and there was no money to meet the bills.

- Your children turned away from God, even though you desperately tried to lead them in the right direction.

- Your children are not making their grades in school.

- Your children are running with the wrong crowd.

- Your friends have turned against you and betrayed you.

- Your dreams have been shattered because the one you love turned to someone else.

- Your body is breaking down, and you are dealing with ongoing pain and doctor visits.

All Things Work Together

Allow me to let you in on a little secret: I have experienced many unpleasant circumstances too. I have lived long enough to know that life can and does throw us curves. But I have also followed my Shepherd for most of my life, and I know He can bring good out of terrible situations.

> And we know that all things work together for good to those who love God, to those who are the called according to His purpose (Romans 8:28).

 How does this verse include the unfortunate circumstances of our lives?

The Holman Commentary states this concerning Romans 8:28:

The promise of this verse [Romans 8:28] is that God orders everything for believers so that all of life's experiences work together for our continual good. Not everything is good in and of itself, but God uses everything for our good (Romans 8:35–36). Jesus taught us that God's sovereign care for and guidance of creation covers even the death of a sparrow and the hairs of our head (Luke 12:6–7, 22–34).[27]

This is the "roll up your sleeves and get on your knees" part of the book. This is a time for you to become a reflecting sheep. Look deeply and intently over the course of your life. Go back as far as you can remember and see how God's goodness and mercy followed you even when things were not as you would have liked. Think back over the good, the bad, and the ugly.

Looking back is good for us if we learn the important lessons, if we will allow the unpleasant circumstances to teach us valuable lessons about ourselves. But if we stay stuck on disappointments and fail to see His goodness and mercy, we are missing out on great spiritual blessings. We look in our rearview mirrors and see those bodyguards following closely behind. That is why we can move forward with confidence.

Two Little Sheep and the Jewelry Sale

When I think of goodness and mercy, I think of the time a friend and I went to a five-dollar jewelry sale at our local hospital. You may be thinking: A jewelry sale at a hospital? Yes, it is something our local hospital hosts twice a year, and we were excited to go. We were running late and wanted to get there before they closed.

I wasn't noticing how fast I was driving, and suddenly I saw a state trooper pull in behind me and turn on his blue and red lights. My heart sank. She said, "Well, you're probably going to get a ticket."

The state trooper came to my window and said, "Let me see your driver's license and your proof of insurance."

---

27 Holman Christian Study Bible (Nashville, TN: Holman Publishers, 2010), 1940.

I handed them out the window to him.

Then he said, "Where are you headed so fast?"

I replied, "To a five-dollar jewelry sale." I noticed a slight grin as he turned to walk to his car. My friend and I sat there discussing how upset Arvy was going to be with me for getting this ticket.

When the trooper came back, I was holding my breath. I just knew he was about to hand me a ticket for speeding as he handed back my license and insurance cards.

Then he said, "Mrs. Dupuy, slow down. You need to arrive at the jewelry sale alive."

"Thank you, thank you!" I said. I wanted to say, "I can't believe you're letting me go," but I wasn't about to bring up the possibility of getting a ticket because I didn't want to remind him.

I cannot explain the relief I felt and the giggles and laughter we had on the way to that sale. I deserved a ticket. But that officer gave me goodness and mercy.

Doesn't God do that for us?

> If we stay stuck on disappointments and fail to see His goodness and mercy, we miss out on great spiritual blessings.

David and His Bodyguards

As we think about the course of David's life and see the goodness and mercy of God, imagine David explaining it like this:

God, over all of my life You have been there. You were there when I was watching my father's sheep. You were there when I wrestled the lion and the bear. You were with me when I stood before a giant with only five smooth stones and a sling—no armor.

You were there when Saul hunted me like a wild animal and I had to hide in caves and watch over my shoulder to keep from being killed.

Lord, You were there when I went to get the Ark of the Covenant and brought it back to Jerusalem. You were with me through every war I fought, and when I begged Your forgiveness for my sins with Bathsheba.

All of my life You have been there, wherever I go, whatever I do. No matter how life treats me, I can't get away from Your goodness and mercy!

When I look over my shoulder, there they are. When I speed up, goodness and mercy are still tracking me down.

When I hide behind the walls of offense, You know where to find me. I just can't get away from Your goodness and mercy!

As the Shepherd's daughter walking in obedience, you can make that claim too: "I just can't get away from Your goodness and mercy; they are following me like two bodyguards. No matter where I go, no matter what I do, they follow me every day, all day long, all the days of my life!"

> Then they cried out to the Lord in their trouble, and He saved them out of their distresses. He brought them out of darkness and the shadow of death and broke their chains in pieces. Oh, that men would give thanks to the Lord for His goodness, and for His wonderful works to the children of men! (Psalm 107:13–15).

Oh, the benefits of being the Shepherd's daughter!

Sheep Homework

1. David brought the Ark of the Covenant home to Jerusalem. It was a glorious day to remember God's goodness and mercy.

2. Read 1 Chronicles 16:7–36. Notice the goodness and mercy of God.

3. Memorize Psalm 106:1: "Oh, give thanks to the Lord, for He is good! For His mercy endures forever."

4. Offer a prayer of thanksgiving to God for His goodness and mercy over the course of your life.

Going Home

I Will Dwell in the House of the Lord Forever

Recite the Twenty-third Psalm.

At the end, add, "Oh, the benefits of being the Shepherd's daughter."

must say there is something about home that makes us want to return. One writer expressed it this way:

> I felt a pang, a strange and inexplicable pang that I had never felt before. It was homesickness. Now, even more than I had earlier when I'd first glimpsed it, I longed to be transported into that quiet little landscape, to walk up the path, to take a key from my pocket and open the cottage door, to sit down by the fireplace, to wrap my arms around myself, and to stay there forever and ever.[28]

I'll never forget a time when our youngest daughter, Anna, went to summer Bible camp in south Alabama. She called and said, "I'm tired, I'm hot, and I'm ready to come home!"

---

28 Alan Bradley, *The Weed That Strings the Hangman's Bag* (New York: Bantam Books, a division of Random House, Inc., 2011), 123.

I said, "Honey, you've only been there one night."

She said, "One night is all I need. There is no air conditioning, I can't get a snack when I want one, my bed is uncomfortable, and there is too much noise down here. Come and get me."

So my mother and I headed off on a Sunday afternoon to pick her up. She was homesick.

 Share a time when you were homesick.

 What is it about home that makes us want to return?

A guy goes into a cafe and when the waitress comes over to take his order, he says, "I'll have runny eggs, burnt toast, and old strong coffee. And I want you to slam the food onto the table and yell at me when you bring it."

The waitress says, "Why should I do that?"

He replies, "I'm homesick."

Sometimes we joke about being homesick, but home is the place we belong. It's a place of love and acceptance where we always have a place at the table. And this is exactly what the sheep says as we come to the last verse, "I will dwell in the house of the Lord forever."

The truer translation is: "I will always be in the presence of the Lord." Heaven! Home!

It's Time to Go Home

Winter is approaching, and for a sheep that means it's time to go home, and he is ready. He longs to go back to the pastures, barns, and corrals of the shepherd.

The flock waits with excitement. It will be a long trek down the mountain from the tableland, but the sheep will follow the shepherd once again through the rough terrain, through the hills and valleys until they approach the place they have excitedly awaited. Home.

Psalm 23 began with "the Lord" and it ends with "the Lord."

What does "the house of the Lord" mean in Psalm 23:6?

Begin and End with YHWH

We learned earlier that some translations help us to recognize God's name by placing His name YHWH in all capital letters: LORD.

What the little sheep explains is that the LORD who created everything and the LORD who is with me every step and in every season of my life is the same LORD who will carry me home. He will never, never leave me, not on the earth and not when I am making my way home to heaven. What a comfort. What joy to know that our LORD begins and ends everything. The sheep at this point is so deeply satisfied within the flock and with His shepherd that he never wants to be anywhere else. The sheep can make this contented statement: "I'll never leave because the Shepherd will never leave me."

David helps us understand by using one word that shows us this isn't temporary housing. The word is *forever*. Forever means "never ending."

 Where will we live forever?

 What does that make your earthly house?

 Where is our homeland according to Philippians 3:20?

The Aging Sheep

Since metaphorically the sheep is now in the winter season of his life, his body isn't what it used to be. He tires easily. But he is ever close to the Good Shepherd and is ready to go home. Home is heaven.

Now he's not so interested in the green pastures and still waters. Maybe he doesn't care as much about changing pastures. Now all he wants is to be with the Shepherd. The sheep understands he was made for more. He is merely flesh and bones, but there is so much more waiting for him.

That's it. He just wants the Shepherd. It's as if he says: Good Shepherd, take my hand and lead me home."

Can't you feel the excitement as the sheep heads back home with the Shepherd? He can't wait to get there. He knows that something better is coming. What about us?

Let not your heart be troubled; you believe in God, believe also in Me. In My Father's house are many mansions; if it were not so, I would have told you. I go to prepare a place for you. And if I go and prepare a place for you, I will come again and receive you to Myself; that where I am, there you may be also. And where I go you know, and the way you know (John 14:1–4).

What does Jesus tell us about home? He makes it clear that "home" is where the Good Shepherd is. Throughout the Old Testament, the House of the Lord is where God dwelt. First, it was the tabernacle. "Let them make Me a sanctuary, that I may dwell among them" (Exodus 25:8). Second, it was the temple. Solomon, David's son, built the temple.

Behold, I propose to build a house for the name of the Lord my God, as the Lord spoke to my father David, saying, "Your son, whom I will set on your throne in your place, he shall build the house for My name" (1 Kings 5:5).

You may wish to read further about the construction of that temple in 1 Kings 6:1–38.

God's House Today

"Do you not know that you are the temple of God and that the Spirit of God dwells in you?" (1 Corinthians 3:16). Where does God dwell? In us! God has always wanted to dwell with His people. He has always provided a house in which to dwell. One day we are going to be with Him in our permanent home.

Heaven Is Home

After these things I looked, and behold, a great multitude which no one could number, of all nations, tribes, peoples, and tongues, standing before the throne and before the Lamb, clothed with white robes, with palm branches in their hands, and crying out with a loud voice, saying, "Salvation belongs to our God who sits on the throne, and to the Lamb!" All the angels stood around the throne and the elders and the four living creatures, and fell on their faces before the throne and worshiped God, saying: "Amen! Blessing and glory and wisdom, thanksgiving and honor and power and might, be to our God forever and ever. Amen" (Revelation 7:9–12).

Read verse 9 again. Who will be in heaven? Heaven is a multicultural place. It won't matter where you lived or how much money you had in your bank account. Everyone will be loved for who they are. God knows that we all bleed the same.

> Home is where the Good Shepherd is.

The Lord recognizes beautiful souls in unity. I believe every tribe and nation is mentioned to show us there will be distinctions and variety. It won't be bland. Just think of the rainbow. How boring would a rainbow be without all of the beautiful colors? Have you ever witnessed a rainbow with the rays of the sun coming forth? It's breathtaking.

That's what heaven will be like. All the people from everywhere coming together and the Son will be shining in, around, and through us. Can you imagine how beautiful this scene will be because of Him, our precious Lamb?

Heaven Is a Place of Celebration

My friends and I love to celebrate just being friends. We can find any excuse to get together because we love spending time laughing and sharing our lives with one another. Every time we get together it is a joyous celebration, but at the end of our time together, we are exhausted. I can only imagine a continuous celebration that never gets tiring. Heaven is a spectacular place. The décor unimaginable!

You may be thinking, how do you know that in heaven we will be celebrating? We know there is a celebration because of what the people there are holding. (See Revelation 7:9.)

Palm branches in scripture were used for festive celebration. In the Old Testament, the people waved them when they were celebrating.

> And you shall take for yourselves on the first day the fruit of beautiful trees, branches of palm trees, the boughs of leafy trees, and willows of the brook; and you shall rejoice before the Lord your God (Leviticus 23:40).

John tells us that Jesus rode into Jerusalem on a donkey a few days before His crucifixion. The people were waving palm branches. Why? Because they were celebrating.

> The next day a great multitude that had come to the feast, when they heard that Jesus was coming to Jerusalem, took branches of palm trees and went out to meet Him, and cried out: "Hosanna! 'Blessed is He who comes in the name of the Lord!' The King of Israel!" (John 12:12–13).

I asked the precious Shepherd's daughters in Haiti, "What do you think the palm branches represent in heaven?" One lady spoke up and said, "I think they are there to use as fans and to cool us from the heat." I am sure she was thinking of the weather and continuous heat in Haiti. I smiled and said, "Why don't we look at Revelation 7:16 for the answer?"

> They shall neither hunger anymore nor thirst anymore; the sun shall not strike them, nor any heat.

She said, "I am so excited to know that it won't be hot." And I replied, "That means we will have no bad hair days in heaven." We all laughed and enjoyed the thoughts of how wonderful it will be to go to heaven.

One of the lines in the classic 1980 hit "Celebration" says: "There's a party going on right here, a celebration to last throughout the year." But I will add, "In heaven it won't be just a year; it will be eternal!"

Heaven Is a Place of Victory

The palm branches are a symbol of victory. They ascribe their victory to God and to Christ. Salvation has a fuller sense of victory for God's people in Revelation 7:10.

The Lord has made known His salvation; His righteousness He has revealed in the sight of the nations. He has remembered His mercy and His faithfulness to the house of Israel; all the ends of the earth have seen the salvation of our God (Psalm 98:2–3).

Heaven Is a Place of Worship

Look back to Revelation 7:10–12.

Salvation belongs to our God who sits on the throne, and to the Lamb!" All the angels stood around the throne and the elders and the four living creatures, and fell on their faces before the throne and worshiped God, saying: "Amen! Blessing and glory and wisdom, thanksgiving and honor and power and might, be to our God forever and ever."

 Describe what you imagine our worship will be like in heaven. Can you image a worship service like the one that awaits us?

Why don't people want to go to worship? Why do they choose other things over worshiping God?

Coin Toss

By the time Bobby arrived, the football game had already started.

"Why are you so late?" asked his friend.

"I couldn't decide between going to church and going to the football game, so I tossed a coin," said Bobby.

"But that shouldn't have taken too long" said the friend.

"Well, I had to toss it thirty-five times."

Bobby wasn't too keen on going to worship, was he?

Wake Up!

A mother went to wake her son for church one Sunday morning. When she knocked on his door, he said, "I'm not going!"

"Why not?" asked his mother.

"I'll give you two good reasons," he said. "One, they don't like me. Two, I don't like them."

His mother replied, "I'll give you two good reasons why you will go to church. One, you're forty-seven years old. Two, you're the preacher!"

No Distractions in Worship There

Worship on earth is quite different from what it will be in heaven. Think about this: While we worship, we deal with our fears, our inhibitions, and all of the daily problems that life brings. We come to worship with burdened hearts—disappointments, aches and pains of a failing body, and even hurtful words from those we love. We deal with hateful looks and prideful attitudes. We are filled with anxiety and confusion. In heaven we will have none of those things.

Our forever home will be a place free of worry, hateful looks, disappointments, betrayal, pride, and pain. There will be no tears, death, or sadness. There will no longer be any worry of finances, long-term illnesses, and broken relationships.

> And God will wipe away every tear from their eyes; there will be no more death, nor sorrow, nor crying. There shall be no more pain, for the former things have passed away (Revelation 21:4).

 What has passed away? What does that mean?

 What won't be in heaven according to this verse?

176

Describe what your forever home will be like physically, mentally, and emotionally?

The Marriage in Heaven

The wife has made herself ready. That means the Bride, the church. And notice what we will be wearing:

> "Let us be glad and rejoice and give Him glory, for the marriage of the lamb has come, and His wife has made herself ready." And to her it was granted to be arrayed in fine linen, clean and bright, for the fine linen is the righteous acts of the saints. Then he said to me, "Write: 'Blessed are those who are called to the marriage supper of the Lamb!'" (Revelation 19:7–9).

Those in fine linen—other versions add white robes—will be all of the people who lived for the Lord on the earth, those covered in the blood of the Lamb.

Can you imagine a place were the best people who ever lived from the beginning of time will be? Can you imagine a place where all the people who love the Lord God and serve Him will be together? Can you imagine a place where only righteous people will dwell?

Name some of the people in the scriptures that you want to meet.

Describe what it will be like not to be subjected to murders, robberies, or any kind of bad news.

Read Revelation 21:8. Who won't be in heaven?

Read Revelation 21:27. What will not enter heaven? Who will enter heaven?

Has your name been written there?

Something Better Is Coming

In *Letters to an American Lady*, C. S. Lewis wrote these words to Mary Willis Shelburne who, being old and frail, was discussing the end of her life.

"There are better things ahead than any we leave behind." [29]

Keep the Fork

I read about a young woman who had been diagnosed with a terminal illness and had been given three months to live. She contacted her preacher to discuss certain aspects of her final wishes. She selected the songs for the service, the scriptures to be read, and the outfit she wanted to be buried in. Everything was in order and the preacher was leaving when the woman suddenly remembered something very important.

"There's one more thing," she said excitedly.

"What's that?"

"This is very important," she continued. "I want to be buried with a fork in my right hand."

The preacher stood looking at the young woman, not knowing quite what to say.

"That surprises you, doesn't it?" the young woman asked.

"Well, to be honest, I'm puzzled," he said.

The young woman explained. "My grandmother once told me this story, and from that time on I have always tried to pass along its message to those I love and those who are in need of encouragement. In all my years of attending socials and dinners, I always remember that when the dishes of the main course were being cleared, someone would inevitably lean over and say, 'Keep your fork.' It was my favorite part because I knew that something better was coming like velvety chocolate cake or deep-dish apple pie. Something wonderful, and with substance!

---

29 Aaron Earls, "7 Things C.S. Lewis Didn't Say," TheWardrobeDoor.com, March 18, 2014. http://thewardrobedoor.com/2014/03/7-things-c-s-lewis-didnt-say.html.

So I just want people to see me there in that casket with a fork in my hand and I want them to wonder, 'What's with the fork?' Then I want you to tell them: 'Keep your fork the best is yet to come.'"

The preacher's eyes welled with tears of joy as he hugged her goodbye. He knew this would be one of the last times he would see her before her death. But he also knew that she had a better grasp of heaven than he did. She had a better grasp of what heaven would be like than many people twice her age and twice as much experience and knowledge. She knew that something better was coming.

At the funeral people were walking by the young woman's casket and they saw the cloak she was wearing and the fork placed in her right hand. Over and over, the preacher heard the question, "What's with the fork?" And over and over he smiled.

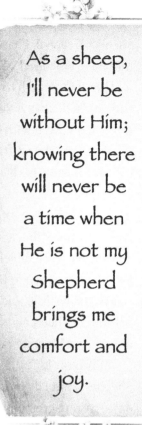

As a sheep, I'll never be without Him; knowing there will never be a time when He is not my Shepherd brings me comfort and joy.

During his message, he told about the conversation he had with the young woman shortly before she died. He also told them about the fork and what it symbolized to her. He told the people that he could not stop thinking about the fork and that they would not be able to stop thinking about it either.

I think he was right. So the next time you "keep your fork," let it remind you ever so gently that the best is yet to come.

Saving the Best for Last

For the Lamb who is in the midst of the throne will shepherd them and lead them to living fountains of waters. And God will wipe away every tear from their eyes" (Revelation 7:17).

Yes, I saved the best for last. Did you notice that He will always be our Shepherd, even in heaven? As a sheep, I'll never be without Him. Just to know that there will never be a time when He is not my Shepherd brings me comfort and joy. It is enough to know that those fountains of living water come from Him and will always flow through my heart, even when the sadness returns. But when I dwell with Him forever, my tears will be forever wiped away.

As David shares the sentiment of his heart, he gives praise to the Lord's divine diligence in the last phrase: *I will dwell in the house of the Lord forever.* Throughout the psalm, the sheep is aware of the shepherd's constant presence and security—there is no lack of any sort. There will always be green pastures and still, clean waters. There will always be new paths and safe summers on the tableland. There will be freedom from fears and the comfort of fresh oil when the flies come to annoy. With the Good Shepherd, the cup is always full, and His goodness and mercy are always following close behind His sheep. No wonder the little sheep is homesick. He just wants to be at home and rest with His Good Shepherd, the darling of heaven.

When my long unsettled journey began, I never knew the closeness of my Shepherd, but I do now. The Shepherd's daughters know that on our darkest days, we must remember to whom we belong. We can ask Him for His direction even in the most minute details. As daughters of the Most High King, let's straighten our crooked little crowns and say to ourselves, "I'm the Shepherd's daughter, and He's all I will ever want."

Oh, the benefits of being the Shepherd's daughter.

Sheep Homework

Research the lyrics to the song "Home," by Chris Tomlin. Jot down the most meaningful phrases to you. What lines remind you of parallels drawn in this chapter?

Conclusion

As I mentioned before, Psalm 23 begins with the Lord and ends with the Lord, and so it was with Dad, my sister, and me.

As Dad lay in his bed in the little room at the assisted-living home, my sister and I sat in the dark. This time it was different.

It came on suddenly and unexpectedly. The director of the cottage came in to be with us. Dad was struggling to breathe. Cindy and I were crying. The director said, "Why don't you talk to your dad, because he can hear you." My sister sat quietly and sobbed.

I choked up and my mind started to swirl as I began to think of what to say. So I went over to my dad, leaned into his ear, and whispered, "Daddy." And then what came out of my mouth surprised me.

I said it again, "Daddy."

> The Lord is my shepherd; I shall not want.
> He makes me to lie down in green pastures;
> He leads me beside the still waters. He restores my soul;
> He leads me in the paths of righteousness for His name's sake.
> Yea, though I walk through the valley of the shadow of death,
> I will fear no evil; for You are with me;
> Your rod and Your staff they comfort me.
> You prepare a table before me in the presence of my enemies;
> You anoint my head with oil; my cup runs over.
> Surely goodness and mercy will follow me all the days of my life;
> And I will dwell in the house of the Lord forever.

As I said the last words of the psalm, Dad took a deep breath, exhaled, and he was gone.

Cindy and I were not ready for that night, but when you know the Shepherd, you are never alone. We cried and embraced for a while. We stayed until everything was finalized and Dad was transported to the funeral home.

We both drove to our homes at 2:00 AM. I will never forget that night. I will always remember that I never felt alone.

Dad's funeral was on Saturday, and I taught my Bible class the next day. I felt the need to honor my Shepherd in my own way. He had been so near and dear to me during these years. Everyone kept saying, "Why don't you wait a few weeks, and then return to class." Those precious ladies were so kind and understanding.

I know that would have been perfectly all right, even the expected thing to do, but I felt such a need to teach that day. I wanted my class to know that the Shepherd we had been studying was real and everything we had learned was being felt by me. Knowing the verses of the Twenty-third Psalm and knowing the Shepherd of the Twenty-third Psalm is what made all the difference.

As the Shepherd's Daughter...

There's no reason to want, because He takes good care of me.
There's no weariness, because He makes me lie down.
There's no reason to be anxious, because He leads me.
There's not a reason to feel hopeless, because He restores me.
I had learned to live for His name's sake.
There's no valley of death, because He is walking me through it.
There is no shadow of grief, because He guides me.
There were no feelings of restlessness or fear, because His presence
    comforted me.
There was the understanding that He has already prepared a
    table for me, and my cup was full to the brim.
There was no reason to be homesick, because I know as His sheep,
    I will dwell in His presence forever, and He will always be the
    Shepherd of this *Shepherd's daughter.*

Oh, the benefits of being the Shepherd's daughter!

Final Lines

It's 2:17 in the afternoon on March 25, 2020, during the Coronavirus epidemic. Tears are flowing as I finish the edits in these last chapters of the book. I always cry when I get to the last chapters, but this time is different.

Our nation is feeling like scared pitiful sheep in need of a shepherd. The future is uncertain, and we seem to fear the unknown.

As I look around in the grocery store at empty shelves, when I read the posts on Facebook, when I listen to the news, I see fearful panicked people acting like sheep without a shepherd. It's unsettling to say the least.

But my tears flow from joy unspeakable in the reassurance of His goodness and mercy and His overflowing cup. My shepherd will *never* leave me or forsake me. He will provide and protect. He will guide and direct me during this season of turmoil. I can rest in His green pasture and know everything will be all right, because He is holding my hand through the day and watching over me when I sleep. That's why He is called the Good Shepherd of my heart!

God's timing is perfect. There are no accidents with God. We are told in the Word, there is a time for every season under heaven. I do believe *The Shepherd's Daughter* is being published at the right time in history to bring us comfort, help, and guidance while we face the unknown. Our Shepherd is YHWH, and He already knows the outcome.

When you run to the Good Shepherd, there's no turning back. He is there with open arms. What a comfort to know that I am safe there!

Debbie Dupuy

(Extra work after chapter 10, page 138)

Going Deeper: Come to the Table

So much of what you do physically happens because you've prepared for it mentally. What if your favorite university coach didn't take the time to prepare for the football season? What would happen if he prepped his team physically but not mentally? Why is mental planning so important in every aspect of our physical lives?

The Enemy Wants the Sheep!

This extra study will take a while to digest. No salads here. You will need a steak knife. We're going to take a deeper look at what is involved in "coming to the table." Jesus is the one who made it possible for us to enjoy a feast.

In Psalm 23:5 David describes a sumptuous pastureland prepared by the Shepherd for His sheep, His beloved. Evil forces are all around, but the Shepherd renders them helpless.

> If he is continuing the shepherd/sheep analogy, he is referring to removing dangerous grasses from their feeding areas and warding off violent animals searching for prey . . .
>
> When three Hebrews—Shadrach, Meshach, and Abednego—were cast into a fiery furnace, they saw God's powerful hand in the presence of their enemies (Daniel 3:13–30). In that situation, God produced an immortal event that has provided continuous encouragement to faithful followers of God. The perpetrators of the evil could only watch in amazement.[30]

Jesus made the promise that we can dine and feast with Him no matter how large the enemy looms. The enemy can do nothing but gaze at the feast.

---

30 Eddie Cloer, D. Min., *Truth for Today Commentary, Psalms 1-50* (Searcy, AR: Resource Publications, 2004), 302.

They will come from the east and the west, from the north and the south, and sit down in the kingdom of God. And indeed there are last who will be first, and there are first who will be last (Luke 13:29–30).

Then He also said to him who invited Him, "When you give a dinner or a supper, do not ask your friends, your brothers, your relatives, nor rich neighbors, lest they also invite you back, and you be repaid. But when you give a feast, invite the poor, the maimed, the lame, the blind. And you will be blessed, because they cannot repay you; for you shall be repaid at the resurrection of the just" (Luke 14:12–14).

In picturesque and parabolic language, Jesus spoke on more than one occasion about feasting and inviting guests to come into the kingdom and sit down at His table. We need to grasp the deep spiritual meaning of the table He has provided. To comprehend Jesus fully, we must realize what He has provided and how He provided it. When we wrap our minds around His great sacrifice and what it means for humanity now, we live differently, fully awake to Him and His provision. So walk along with me, and come to His table.

And I bestow upon you a kingdom, just as My Father bestowed one upon Me, that you may eat and drink at My table in My kingdom, and sit on thrones judging the twelve tribes of Israel (Luke 22:29–30).

The Lamb of the Old Testament

Jesus was perfectly prepared to be our perfect Savior. His Father stood ready to send Him to earth. But Israel had to learn many lessons about sacrifice and purity before they could understand the redeeming power of the blood of Jesus. That process took fifteen hundred years.

- Two lambs, one in the morning and one in the evening, were offered as whole burnt offerings to demonstrate total devotion. They were a sweet-smelling offering to God (Exodus 29:38–42).

- The Jews knew about the coming one who would be brought as a "lamb led to the slaughter" (Isaiah 53:7).

- The Passover was a feast celebrating God's deliverance of the Israelites from Egyptian bondage. The blood of a lamb was spread on the two doorposts and the lintel of each of the Israelite houses (Exodus 12:7).

- The blood of those lambs was a foreshadowing of the sacrifice Jesus as a substitute for us (Exodus 12:13; Matthew 26:28).

In the broader view of our Psalm 23:5 text and preparing the table, what was Jesus asking them to do in Matthew 26:28?

Who made Passover preparations ahead of time?

What did the disciples do?

Jesus was inviting His disciples to come to His table. He had already made preparations. He was preparing Himself to be the "feast at the table."

And as they were eating, Jesus took bread, blessed and broke *it*, and gave *it* to the disciples and said, "Take, eat; this is My body." Then He took the cup, and gave thanks, and gave *it* to them, saying, "Drink from it, all of you. For this is My blood of the new covenant, which is shed for many for the remission of sins. But I say to you, I will not drink of this fruit of the vine from now on until that day when I drink it new with you in My Father's kingdom" (Matthew 26:26–29).

To what feast was Jesus referring?

What did the bread and the cup represent?

Of whose death was Jesus speaking?

Washing Feet at the Table

As the feast progressed, Jesus was preparing to be denied by Peter and betrayed by Judas, both in preparation for His crucifixion.

Immediately after Jesus inaugurated the Lord's supper, He announced that the betrayer was with him at the table. Then there arose a dispute among them as to which should be considered the greatest. After Jesus quelled that argument, He announced that He was bestowing on them a kingdom "that you may eat and drink at my table in My kingdom" (Luke 22:30). Then He told Peter, "Satan has asked for you, that he may sift you as wheat" (Luke 22:31). Then Jesus said, "I tell you, Peter, the rooster shall not crow this day before you will deny three times that you know Me" (Luke 22:34).

Jesus is indeed the Good Shepherd. A short time before, He was eating the Passover with Peter. After that He instituted the Lord's supper—His broken body and His shed blood for the remission of sins. Then He assumed the role of a slave. He washed Peter's feet, the feet of the man who would that night deny that he knew the Lord. That should assure us of His love for us, even when we sin against Him. Jesus knows we will stray from the path of righteousness, and He is prepared to help penitent ones to overcome their weaknesses. Oh, what a Good Shepherd we follow!

How would you feel eating with a denier and a betrayer?

What does Jesus' servitude to His disciples tell you about His love and His readiness to forgive?

Describe the preparations that Jesus was going through mentally.

The Loneliness of Gethsemane

Before Jesus left the upper room with His disciples to go out to the Mount of Olives, they sang a hymn (Matthew 26:30). There He urged Peter, James, and John to watch with Him. Then He prayed to His Father; He struggled with the sins of humanity. Perhaps He also contended with Satan for His very life, for "an angel appeared to Him from heaven, strengthening Him" (Luke 22:43). He went once more to urge His disciples to watch, but Judas came from among the soldiers.

Immediately he went up to Jesus and said, "Greetings, Rabbi!" and kissed Him. But Jesus said to him, "Friend, why have you come?" Then they came and laid hands on Jesus and took Him (Matthew 26:49–50).

While Jesus was being questioned by Caiaphas, Peter was outside being questioned by a servant girl as to his association with Jesus. Peter denied Jesus three times. Then the rooster crowed, as Jesus had said (Matthew 26:34).

And the Lord turned and looked at Peter. And Peter remembered the word of the Lord, how He had said to him, "Before the rooster crows, you will deny Me three times." So Peter went out and wept bitterly (Luke 22:61–62).

At the Passover table, in Gethsemane, and now in the presence of the high priest, scribes, and elders, Jesus was preparing a feast for His followers.

Then the high priest tore his clothes and said, "What further need do we have of witnesses? You have heard the blasphemy! What do you think?" And they all condemned Him to be deserving of death. Then some began to spit on Him, and to blindfold Him, and to beat Him, and to say to Him, "Prophesy!" And the officers struck Him with the palms of their hands (Mark 14:63–65).

What did the high priest do when Jesus told him He was the Christ?

Why did the Jewish court determine that Jesus was guilty of blasphemy?

What physical torture did Jesus' enemies place upon Him because of His claim to be the Christ?

Although His Jewish enemies did not know it, they were creating an environment for Jesus to prepare a table for His followers.

That preparation continued with the abuse, beating, and the death sentence in the judgment hall of Pontus Pilate, the Roman governor.

Pilate answered and said to them again, "What then do you want me to do with Him whom you call the King of the Jews?" So they cried out again,

"Crucify Him!" Then Pilate said to them, "Why, what evil has He done?" But they cried out all the more, "Crucify Him!" So Pilate, wanting to gratify the crowd, released Barabbas to them; and he delivered Jesus, after he had scourged Him, to be crucified. Then the soldiers led Him away into the hall called Praetorium, and they called together the whole garrison. And they clothed Him with purple; and they twisted a crown of thorns, put it on His head, and began to salute Him, "Hail, King of the Jews!" Then they struck Him on the head with a reed and spat on Him; and bowing the knee, they worshiped Him. And when they had mocked Him, they took the purple off Him, put His own clothes on Him, and led Him out to crucify Him (Mark 15:12–20).

Pilate knew He was not guilty, but because of the turmoil his verdict elicited, he scourged Jesus and delivered Him to be crucified. The governor's own soldiers carried out the execution.

What demand did Jesus' Jewish accusers make of Governor Pilate?

When Pilate asked, "What has He done," what did His accusers say?

Why did Pilate free a known criminal instead of releasing Jesus?

What did Pilate do to Jesus before he delivered Him for crucifixion?

Describe the environment created by mocking soldiers as Jesus prepared His table for us.

As the nails were driven into His hands and feet, Jesus was among Jewish and Roman enemies. The sins of humanity were upon Him, and His Father was about to turn away from Him. His preparation of a bountiful table was not apparent to anyone except deity. Six hours later, Jesus announced the success of His mission: "It is finished." With the crucifixion, Jesus had finished the work. The resurrection three days later validated His deity. He was fully prepared to set His table.

The debt of sin had been paid in full. Neither the scoffers nor His disciples understood that—but we do. Thank God, we understand it!

Resurrection!

Jesus used the occasion of the Passover to initiate the memorial feast of His body and His blood. He agonized in the garden because of the negligence of His disciples and the sins of humanity. He took the abuse of the His own people at the house of the high priest. He was tortured after Pilate's "not guilty but crucify Him anyway" verdict. Finally, He agonized on the cross for three hours. All those things occurred within a twenty-four-hour period. Had He been in the presence of His enemies? Yes. Had He prepared His table? Yes. What kind of table? A table of hope; a table of love; a table of forgiveness. He died, He was buried, and He arose, just as the scriptures said He would. He is truly the Son of God—God in the flesh (John 1:14). The resurrection validated His identity. What a table; what a feast; what a message!

A Feast by the River

Peter went back to what he knew best: fishing. It seems we always go back to our old ways when we don't know what else to do. He was lost in sorrow. Peter had walked on water with the Lord but was later drowning in a sea of regret. He couldn't deny his denial. The resurrection was powerful, but it did not eliminate Judas' noose or Peter's crowing rooster. So back to fishing.

Peter and his friends fished all night and caught nothing. The next morning, Jesus was on the shore, but the fishermen did not know who He was. "Cast the net on the right side of the boat, and you will find some." They cast and drew in a multitude of fish. "It is the Lord," John announced. Peter jumped into the sea.

As the disciples were about to drag the net ashore, Jesus asked for some fish to cook for breakfast. Then they shared a feast of bread and fish.

Although that is not the table Jesus prepared in His suffering and death, the fellowship that ensued was a product of that table. The disciples had forsaken Him; Peter had denied Him. The meal they shared was much greater than fish and bread. The defeater of hell and death, the only perfect man, the one who reversed the curse, the ruler of heaven invited His friends to sit down and have a bite to eat. Think of it. That was after He was crucified. Right there on the shore of the Sea of Galilee the devil and his tempters got a small glimpse of the table Jesus was preparing while they were gloating over His "defeat." And yes, He exceled in the presence of His enemies. No one was more grateful than Peter.

Table of Remembrance Each First Day of the Week

Since that first Pentecost after the resurrection of our Lord, Christians have met on the first day of the week to remember the table Jesus prepared for us. The loneliness, suffering, and shame He endured for our "table" of instruction, fellowship, and forgiveness are memorialized by simple emblems: unleavened bread and fruit of the vine.

When we come to the Lord's table and partake of the bread and fruit of the vine, it is a communion of the body and blood of Christ, a feast of thanksgiving for His love and care. As we sit at His table, we participate in a feast of remembrance for all He has given us.

Do we fully appreciate what it cost Him to prepare that table for us? When I ask that question, I quickly turn my mind to the table each first day of the week. The Christians in the first century came together each first day of the week to break bread and remember Jesus' death (Acts 20:7). Has that solemn feast become just another ritual to us? Are we truly examining ourselves as we remember what it cost Him to prepare that table for us (1 Corinthians 11:28)?

The Great Banquet Feast in Heaven

The story of the table is not over. The ultimate pastureland is prepared by our Shepherd. John 14:3 records the words of Jesus letting us know that He has gone to "prepare a place," and that He will come again for us.

David's shepherd of Psalm 23 prepared the tableland for his sheep. But that pasture holds no comparison to the splendor of heaven, which is far beyond our comprehension. Only our Good Shepherd who knows His sheep can prepare such a place for us. And some day He will return for us. Can't you hear Him say, "Come, for all things are now ready" (Luke 14:17)?

Have you made your reservation?

A Mother's Story

My young daughter and I were about to see a play about Jesus. She was all dressed up in her Sunday dress, matching purse, and new shoes.

As the play started, she saw the cast of actors coming on stage and in an excited whisper said, "Mommy, there's Jesus!" He was playing with the children on stage and she wanted to know why she couldn't go up and play with Jesus too.

My response was, "Honey, this is only a play. He's only an actor. This isn't real."

"Okay," she said, "but will you lift me up so I can see Jesus and He can see my new dress?"

During the scene of Jesus praying in the Garden of Gethsemane, soldiers came barging in yelling and screaming. My daughter became so frightened that she turned her head, buried her face into my chest, and began to cry. Again I told her, "It's okay, honey. This is only a play. Those are only actors. It isn't real." So we kept watching.

Later, the soldiers grabbed Jesus, threw Him against the cross, picked up their hammers and nails and bam, bam, bam! She screamed to the top of her lungs, "Noooooooo! They are killing my Jesus!" She cried so loud and so long that I had to rush her out of the auditorium.

I took her into a room with a large TV screen where she could finish watching the play. And I assured her that Jesus would come back to life. But she would not be consoled until she could see Him herself.

Many people were in the auditorium that day. Like me, they had all gone to see a play, only actors—it wasn't real. But when I saw the gospel through the eyes of a child, the gospel became real once again.

Has the gospel become just another story for us? Has it lost its appeal? Maybe we need to pray for childlike faith so we can be moved with the excitement of what He has done and prepared for us. When He says "come to the table," we want to recognize all that Jesus has done. And we don't want to miss the feast, so bring your steak knife. There will be so much for His sheep to "chew on" for all eternity.

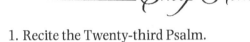

Sheep Homework

1. Recite the Twenty-third Psalm.

2. Memorize 1 Corinthians 15:4.

3. Record the benefits of being the Shepherd's daughter.

4. How has this study changed your view of what it means to come to the table?

5. Share your faith in Jesus and the benefits with someone else.

6. How can you grasp more intently the preparations involved for you to "come to the table"?

CPSIA information can be obtained
at www.ICGtesting.com
Printed in the USA
BVHW070355200922
647263BV00004B/11